Praise for the Real People,

"Jodie's Bible studies are some of my favorite resources! Her insightful and practical application of Scripture keeps her studies at the top of my list. Anyone who uses this Bible study will feel closer to God and better understand his truth."

KAT ARMSTRONG, preacher, author of *The In-Between Place*, and cofounder of The Polished Network

"Each weekly lesson includes a practice session to help us apply gleaned wisdom for navigating our own crossroads. Jodie's studies move us toward transformative biblical literacy and an action-packed faith that lives what's learned."

SUE EDWARDS, professor at Dallas Theological Seminary and author of the Discover Together Bible Study series

"This study will stretch and challenge you as Jodie guides with wisdom and practical application each step of the way. I deeply value how Jodie refuses to simply fill our minds with information about the Bible—she consistently pursues the 'So what?' question so we are stirred to action."

NANCY BEACH, leadership coach with the Slingshot Group and author of *Gifted to Lead*

"Niznik's highly practical invitations toward spiritual disciplines further root me in the powerful message that I am loved, God has a plan for my life, and obedience brings joy. This will be a perfect Bible study addition to any ministry longing to deepen women's connection to God."

MARY DEMUTH, author of over forty books, including *Into the Light*

"Each week is filled with outstanding biblical teaching as well as opportunities to consider how these truths apply to our lives. I especially appreciate that Niznik incorporates spiritual practices that enable us to delve deeper into our relationship with the Lord."

SISSY MATHEW, spiritual formation and teaching pastor at Irving Bible Church

REAL PEOPLE, REAL FAITH BIBLE STUDIES

Choose: A Study of Moses for a Life That Matters

*Crossroads: A Study of Esther and Jonah
for Boldly Responding to Your Call*

*Trust: A Study of Joseph for Persevering
Through Life's Challenges*

*Journey: A Study of Peter for Stumbling
Toward Jesus's Extravagant Grace*

A
REAL PEOPLE
REAL FAITH
BIBLE STUDY

TRUST

A Study of Joseph for Persevering Through Life's Challenges

JODIE NIZNIK

KREGEL
PUBLICATIONS

Trust: A Study of Joseph for Persevering Through Life's Challenges
© 2021 by Jodie Niznik

Published by Kregel Publications, a division of Kregel Inc., 2450 Oak Industrial Dr. NE, Grand Rapids, MI 49505.

All rights reserved. No part of this book may be reproduced, stored in a retrieval system, or transmitted in any form or by any means—electronic, mechanical, photocopy, recording, or otherwise—without written permission of the publisher, except for brief quotations in reviews.

Distribution of digital editions of this book in any format via the internet or any other means without the publisher's written permission or by license agreement is a violation of copyright law and is subject to substantial fines and penalties. Thank you for supporting the author's rights by purchasing only authorized editions.

All Scripture quotations, unless otherwise indicated, are from the Holy Bible, New International Version®, NIV®. Copyright © 1973, 1978, 1984, 2011 by Biblica, Inc.™ Used by permission of Zondervan. All rights reserved worldwide. www.zondervan.com. The "NIV" and "New International Version" are trademarks registered in the United States Patent and Trademark Office by Biblica, Inc.™

Scripture quotations marked ESV are from the ESV® Bible (The Holy Bible, English Standard Version®), copyright © 2001 by Crossway, a publishing ministry of Good News Publishers. Used by permission. All rights reserved.

Scripture quotations marked NLT are from the Holy Bible, New Living Translation, copyright © 1996, 2004, 2015 by Tyndale House Foundation. Used by permission of Tyndale House Publishers, Inc., Carol Stream, Illinois 60188. All rights reserved.

Cataloging-in-Publication Data is available from the Library of Congress.

ISBN 978-0-8254-4672-6, print
ISBN 978-0-8254-7800-0, epub

Printed in the United States of America
21 22 23 24 25 26 27 28 29 30 / 5 4 3 2 1

To my forever soul friend, Cheri:
you show me what it means to trust God
in every circumstance—
thank you for always pointing me to Jesus first

CONTENTS

•• • ● ● •••

WHY JOSEPH AND WHY NOW?

•••••••

It's been a season of uncertainty around my house, and I'm guessing it might have been the same for you. But even if you aren't in a season of uncertainty, I can sadly promise that one is coming. It's just the way life is. As I've prayed about how to handle my tumultuous time, God kept bringing me back to Joseph. Talk about a man who had to move through uncertainty! His entire life got upended. He woke up one morning wrapped in the best style of the day, thinking life would turn out one way, and went to sleep that night as a slave, knowing nothing would be the same.

How did he handle this unexpected and unwelcome turn of events? By faithfully trusting in God. Every step of the way, Joseph chose trust again and again. And even if he did have a pity party that we aren't privy to, it seems he got over it quickly. Because what we do see is that Joseph kept doing the next right thing. Day after day. Even when the right things weren't done in return. Joseph chose trust.

Trust can be difficult when things feel uncertain and out of control. But journeying with Joseph has shown me that trust is not impossible, and I believe his story will show you the same. How can you choose trust in uncertainty? By remembering who God is. By knowing that God is still working, and he works all things for good.

I pray that as you journey through this study your trust in God will grow. No matter where you are or what you're going through, God is good, and he is with you. You can trust him.

—Jodie

WHAT TO EXPECT IN THIS STUDY

• • ● • • •

Practice Sections

Each week our lesson will start with a short practice section. These practices are an opportunity for you to take some of the concepts we are learning and live them out, perhaps in a way you've never tried before. These practices won't take a lot of time, but they may require some planning. Therefore, we will start each week's lesson with the practice section. Prayerfully read it through and then make a plan to try the suggested activities.

You may discover something you really love in these little sections—something that brings new life into your relationship with the Lord. You may also discover that some of these exercises will take effort. Some may be hard for you to do and others may be easy, even fun! They will all help you stretch and grow. Growth almost always brings the spiritual fruit of a changed life. For me, that makes any effort totally worth it.

Pacing Your Study

Each week of this study includes a practice for the week and four study sessions. You are welcome to tackle as much of the week's material as you like on any given day. However, I suggest giving yourself five days to complete the week's work, and I have marked the sections accordingly. If you break it into these chunks, the study shouldn't take you more than thirty minutes to do each day. However, if you are a researcher or extensive reflective thinker, you may want to set aside more time for each day's study.

In general, you will find the days broken down as follows:

Day one will be reading about and planning for the practice activity.

Days two through five will be reading Scripture and answering the questions in this study guide.

If you start running behind (we all have those weeks), you may have to pick and choose which questions you want to answer. My advice is to make the Scripture reading your first priority. Then if you have time, scan through the questions to see which ones you want to answer.

As is usually the case, the higher the investment, the greater the return. When we collaborate with Jesus by inviting him into our lives and spending time with him, we experience life transformation. As your life is transformed, you will find it looking more and more like the life God designed you to live. So make every effort to arrange your days so that you can regularly spend time with Jesus.

FAVORED TO FORSAKEN

Day 1
Practice—Serving in Secret

Joseph was the favorite. His father, Jacob, cherished and loved him more than his eleven brothers. This made him the favorite son of the favorite wife. (Yes, Jacob had more than one wife. We will get to that soon.) You can already see there are going to be issues, can't you? Playing favorites only feels good to one person—the favored one. Competition, jealousy, and hatred become ripe for the picking for everyone else.

We know this feeling, don't we? We've all been overlooked, passed over, and picked last—or not at all. All while the people around us seem to get what we wanted and hoped for. Favor. Favor never seems to fall on us, just everyone else.

But I wonder if getting overlooked is sometimes just a function of how we interpret a particular situation. Perhaps those feelings of rejection sting us so deeply that they blind us to noticing how often we actually are being given preference. Whether that has been true in our lives or not, here's what we do know: favoritism is dangerous. It's a false system built with an arbitrary measuring stick. And it's tempting to grab at the chance to be the favored one whenever the opportunity presents itself.

I do it more than I'd like to admit. From skipping the long line when the cashier ushers me into the newly opened one to making sure my boss publicly attributes the good work to me. I have a confession: I like being preferred over others. I like hearing things such as, "We don't do this for just anyone," "This is special—just for you," "You're better at this than he is," or "I'd rather spend time with you than her." These statements of favor and preferential treatment are like dopamine hits for my brain. They make me feel good, and I suspect they do the same for you.

It's not that it's wrong to be recognized or celebrated; it's when longing for favor becomes our driving motivation that we get ourselves into trouble. When this happens, no amount of recognition is actually good enough. It all falls short. That's the problem with being favored for a moment—it only lasts for a moment. And then it's gone and we're just like everyone else again.

Here's the good news: God doesn't play the favorites game. He looks upon each of us with the same loving gaze. We know this for many reasons, but namely because he sent Jesus to die for our sins when none of us deserved it (Romans 5:8). And we are saved by our faith in Jesus, not by anything we do or don't do (Ephesians 2:8–9). There's no earning God's love—and this is solid evidence to us that he doesn't have favorites. Playing favorites is something humans made up—and like all things we make up that are outside of God's best for us, it never turns out well. Joseph, as you will see in this lesson, is a prime example of just how damaging favoritism can be to not only one person but entire families.

This week, to try to diminish our natural desire to be recognized and favored, we're going to seek to serve others in secret. This is actually a practice Jesus encouraged when he said, "When you give to the needy, do not let your left hand know what your right hand is doing, so that your giving may be in secret" (Matthew 6:3–4). God knows that when we get noticed for our good deeds, that recognition can start to become our motivation instead of him being our motivation. Serving in secret is one way we can keep our hearts in check and serve God simply because he's God.

To do this practice, start each day with the simple prayer, "Lord, show me who you want me to bless today." Then keep your eyes open for opportunities and be ready to serve others as you feel the Lord leads. It could be that you hear of a need and make a strategic plan for how you can quietly help without being noticed. Or perhaps it's more spur of the moment, like helping a stranger or joyfully allowing that car to cut in front of you after you've waited in the long traffic line. I'm not sure what the Lord will place in your path, but I feel confident you will have multiple opportunities to serve and bless others. The goal is to do these acts of service without being noticed, so if for some reason you get caught or someone tries to recognize you, just give credit to God and quietly move on.

In the end, we are seeking to let God, not us, get the glory for the good. I'll never forget when my family had a need, and someone left the right gift card for the right amount in our mailbox. I've never discovered who that person was, and while I'm still incredibly curious, I'm glad I don't know. That person serving my family in secret helped me see God more clearly. If I knew who it was, I would have been tempted to marvel at how nice they were. Instead, I marveled at God and was reminded that he saw my family and would care for us. And I'm sure it also did my secret server good to not be known. Having us swoon over them might have gone straight to their head; it would have mine. Really, everyone wins when we allow God to use us in this way. Have fun on your adventure of secret service this week.

- Spend a few minutes in prayer asking God to help you see places and people he may want you to serve. Write down anything that comes to mind.

- If a situation or person comes to mind, write a plan of action for how you will serve them in secret this week. Be as specific as possible, including the dates you will do things.

Pray, "Lord, show me who you want
me to bless today." Then keep your
eyes open for opportunities to bless
others without being noticed.

Day 2
The Dreamer

The story of Joseph is found in the book of Genesis, the first book of the Bible. Genesis tells the story of God's perfect creation, humankind's consistent choice of their own ways over God's ways, and the coming of Jesus to reconcile our waywardness. Genesis also makes it clear that Jesus would enter the world through God's people, the Jews. Joseph's story occupies thirteen of the fifty chapters in Genesis, which is more space than any other person receives in this book. His story has much to teach us about trusting in God even when things go terribly wrong, because there is much that goes terribly wrong for Joseph.

To start with, Joseph was born into a family that could dominate the tabloids. His father, Jacob, who is also called Israel, had two wives and they were sisters, which is a whole other fascinating story of double-crossing and deception.

If you want to know more about the story of how Jacob wound up married to sisters, read Genesis 29.

These two sisters, Leah and Rachel, were fiercely competitive and jealous of each other. Leah, the older sister and first wife, was jealous because Jacob loved Rachel more than her. And Rachel was jealous because Leah had child after child while Rachel was left behind in her barrenness. Their answer to this competition was to throw their female servants at Jacob to have more children.

While this was a common cultural practice, it doesn't make much sense to us today. However, in their culture, children were everything and brought great honor to the family. Thus, they would do anything to have children—the more the better. Women who had no children felt deep shame and were often stigmatized by the community.

So now we have four women having, or trying to have, children with the same man. Baby after baby came on the scene and this dysfunctional family soon amassed ten sons and one daughter. Finally, Rachel's long-held dream came true and she had a baby boy, declaring, "God has taken away my disgrace" (Genesis 30:23). She named him Joseph, which means "May the LORD add to me another son" (verse 24). Joseph, born to the favorite wife, quickly became the favorite son. And as we explored in the practice section, playing favorites never goes well. Joseph's older brothers took serious issue with the preferential treatment given to their baby brother. And Joseph, in his immaturity, seemed to relish being daddy's boy.

Rachel's prayer for another son was finally answered, and she gave birth to Joseph's younger brother, Benjamin. But sadly, while she was giving birth, she died (Genesis 35:16–18). This leaves Jacob without his beloved wife and Joseph without his mother.

Read Genesis 37:1–11.

1. Write down all the things you learn about Joseph and his family from verses 1–4. Especially note the dysfunctional dynamics of playing favorites starting to emerge. Consider the actions of Joseph, Israel, and the brothers.

The New International Version Bible translation says Jacob made Joseph an "ornate robe" (verse 3). This probably conjures up images of a multicolored coat-like garment. And while this robe potentially fits that imagery, the original Hebrew word isn't quite clear about the colorfulness of the robe. A more specific translation would be to describe the robe as reaching from his palms to his soles. It was long sleeved and long hemmed, which meant it was not suited for working in the fields as a sheepherder. You could call the robe ornate because it was impractical for working. To work as a sheepherder, one would wear a much shorter garment that would allow ease of movement. Regardless of what the robe actually looked like, what the "ornate" description reveals is that Joseph was likely given the preferential status of an overseer instead of being expected to do the work of a sheepherder in the fields with his brothers.

2. Briefly describe the first dream Joseph told his brothers about (verses 5–7). While we can't know for certain what Joseph was really thinking or feeling, imagine for a moment what it might have been like to be him, favored by your father and despised by your siblings. Why do you think he told them about the dream, especially considering how they treated him (verse 4)? Why do you think the brothers reacted as they did?

3. Joseph had a second dream and again told his brothers and father about it (verses 9–11). Why do you think Joseph told them about this dream, especially considering how it went when he told them about the first dream? How did his father react to this dream?

I'm not sure if Joseph was oblivious or just immature, but he seemed to keep going back for more. In these verses we learn that the brothers hated Joseph and spoke unkindly to him. Three times the text tells us they hated him (verses 4, 5, and 8) and then verse 11 caps it off by telling us they were "jealous of him."

Jealousy happens when we become dissatisfied with what we have in comparison to what someone else has. The brothers seemed to be jealous of Joseph for exactly this reason.

4. Have you ever been in a situation where you were consistently treated unkindly by someone (perhaps because they were jealous of you)? What happened and how did you respond? Did you play any part in further instigating this situation? (Keep in mind, if you were or are in an abusive situation, you did not and do not ever deserve this kind of treatment. This question is meant to ask if you played any role in furthering jealousy—like Joseph did in flaunting his dreams to his brothers, who already mistreated and hated him.) Is there something you could have done differently that might have helped mitigate what was happening?

Read Acts 13:44–52.

5. In this passage Paul and Barnabas were preaching the gospel of Jesus to the people in Antioch and the Jews became jealous of their success. What did the Jews do? How did Paul and Barnabas respond?

Began to contradict paul, reviling him.

spoke out boldly

They didn't ~~to~~ stay there trying to convince them. That would have

6. What can you learn from this passage that you could apply to the next time you're being treated unkindly due to jealousy?

distracted them from the mission.

· We don't know what Joseph's motives were but we do know the results.

PRACTICE REMINDER

Pray, "Lord, show me who you want
me to bless today." Then keep your
eyes open for opportunities to bless
others without being noticed.

DAY 3
A Fateful Errand

Read Genesis 37:12–22.

In this scene, the brothers left to graze the flocks in Shechem,
which was about fifty miles from where they lived.

7. According to verse 14, why did Israel send Joseph to the
   brothers? Considering what we learned about Joseph in
   verse 2, why do you think Israel thought Joseph was the
   right person to send on this errand?

   *To see if it is well w/ the
   brother's + the flock*

8. Joseph arrived in Shechem and didn't find his brothers
   (verses 14–16). What happened that helped Joseph find
   where his brothers went? What do you think the odds were
   of Joseph running into a man in an open field who knew
   that the brothers had moved on and also overheard where
   they were going? What do you think this means about
   God's involvement in Joseph's story?

   *God is intentionally
   @ work even amidst
   painful circumstances.*

Joseph moved on to Dothan to find his brothers, which was roughly another fifteen miles farther away. When he found them, they saw him coming in the distance and recognized that it was him. This is another reason why it's plausible that Joseph's robe was distinct and perhaps colorful, as it was easy to recognize from some distance away.

9. When the brothers saw Joseph, what did they decide to do (verses 18–22)? What did Reuben do to try to thwart the murder? According to Genesis 35:23, what do you learn about Reuben and why do you think this made him more inclined to try to save Joseph?

They conspired to kill him. They initially planned to kill him + throw him in a pit. They planned to lie + say he got killed by an animal.
Reuben - " Shed no blood but throw him into the pit."
Oldest - leader, sense of responsibility.

We have no way of knowing, but I would guess when the brothers saw Joseph coming, one of them threw out the comment about killing him almost as a joke. "Hey, here comes that dreamer. You know what we should do—just get rid of him." Ha ha. And then, they all looked at each other and decided it wasn't such a bad idea after all. The plan spiraled out of control and they found themselves plotting his murder and the cover-up.

If it happened this way, it is what psychologists commonly call groupthink. In simple terms, it is when a group of people make an irrational decision that they would almost never make on their own. Reuben tried to step in and stop the group, but he wasn't fully successful. He seemed to know the right thing to do, but he didn't know how to make it happen.

10. Thinking back over your life, when have you been in a situation where others wanted to do something that you knew wasn't right? Briefly describe what happened. Were you able to impact the situation? Why or why not? If you could go back and do things differently, what would you do?

11. Since it's likely we won't find ourselves in a situation where we groupthink our way into plotting a murder, what are some more plausible groupthink situations you might find yourself in today (for example, a conversation that turns to tearing someone down)? According to Ephesians 6:10–18, what are some practical ways you can prepare yourself to stand firm in these situations? If you already do some of these things, how have they been helpful?

Call to mind vs. about speech
ask questions... does this
promote unity?

If you have found success in curbing a potentially destructive situation, take a few minutes to share this encouraging story with your small group. Taking care, of course, to not share details that would be hurtful to someone. We all need the reminder that we can stand firm against the enemy when we are tempted. And we can find loving ways to help others do the same. First Corinthians 16:13–14 sums it up well: "Be on your guard; stand firm in the faith; be courageous; be strong. Do everything in love."

If just one of the brothers had done this well, it would have saved heartache, grief, and a lifetime of pain for multiple people.

PRACTICE REMINDER

Pray, "Lord, show me who you want
me to bless today." Then keep your
eyes open for opportunities to bless
others without being noticed.

Day 4
Sold as a Slave

Read Genesis 37:23–25.

This is where Joseph's story takes a dark turn.

12. What did the brothers do to Joseph in verses 23–24? Pause and imagine this scene where Joseph, who was seventeen, was attacked by his older brothers, who were grown men. What do you think they might have said to Joseph as they took his robe and threw him into the cistern? What do you think Joseph might have said to them?

Betrayal, terrified, abandonded

"Why?! Please stop. please!"

Hard hearts ·TRAUMATIC

⭐ The importance of seperating yourself from the group + looking directly to God vs. others for direction

Cisterns were common in this part of the world. They were large man-made reservoirs that held water in the rainy season. This cistern was obviously deep enough that Joseph could not get himself out of it without assistance. This whole act of stripping Joseph of his coat and throwing him into the cistern is full of aggression and violence.

"When we read that his brothers 'stripped' his robe from him, this is the same word as would be used for skinning an animal. This was a violent attack. The term for throwing him into the dry cistern is the term used for discarding a dead body."

—Nancy Guthrie[1]

13. After the brothers threw him into the cistern, they sat down to eat. Imagine this part of the scene. Read Genesis 42:21, which is how the brothers recalled this account about twenty years later. Of course, we don't know exactly what happened, but it's often helpful to use our imaginations to engage in Scripture reading. Based on the verse, what do you think Joseph might have been feeling and possibly even yelling from the bottom of the cistern? What do you think the brothers' temperaments were, and what might they have discussed while they ate?

To be able to eat after such a traumatic event reveals an incredible hardness of hearts.

14. Recall from Genesis 37:4 that the brothers "could not speak a kind word" to Joseph. Do you think Joseph believed his life was in real danger, or do you think he believed this was more of the same bullying he had certainly endured in the past? What do you think might have made this incident feel different?

15. Where do you think God was in this whole scene? Why do you think he allowed all this to happen to Joseph and didn't step in to stop it? (It's OK to wrestle with this and come up with more questions than answers. We won't ever have all the answers, but hopefully, as we continue in the study, we will see some of the reasons why he allowed this.)

Joseph is completely vulnerable and at the mercy of his brothers. Even if he thought this was just more of the same sibling rivalry, he was still physically hurt (at least with a few bumps and bruises) from being thrown into the cistern. I'm guessing he wondered when they would let him out. And he probably also started planning the report he would give their father.

What happens here goes well beyond childhood sibling rivalry, though. The brothers had allowed their jealousy to grow to a place where they were taking destructive action. The first thing they did was strip Joseph of his special coat—the one thing that made him stand out as the favorite. Think about that for a minute. When we feel jealousy, in our worst moments, what do we secretly want to happen? We want that one thing to be taken away from that person. This is why jealousy can be so destructive—and it's why it is a sin. When we allow ourselves to become embroiled with jealousy, we don't just want what the other person has, we want it to be taken from them.

If we can learn anything from these brothers, it is that we must be vigilant to root out jealousy in our lives. There is nothing good that comes from harboring this ugly emotion and allowing it to grow and fester.

16. Read Galatians 5:16–26. According to this passage, jealousy is one of the "acts of the flesh." What does verse 16 say is the antidote to the acts of the flesh? Which aspect of the fruit of the Spirit listed in verses 22 and 23 do you think would be most helpful in disarming jealous feelings? While the fruit of the Spirit is given by the Holy Spirit to us, there are also things we can do to cultivate this fruit in our lives. Considering this, what are some practical ways you can cultivate the aspect you identified to help you disarm jealousy?

What ways can you better cultivate the work of the HS

- pray, actively serve.

... "walk by the Spirit and you will not gratify the desires of the flesh"

love - want what's best/good for another

17. Is there anyone you currently feel any aspect of jealousy toward? Honestly assess why you feel this way (feel free to write in code). Take a few minutes to journal a prayer ask-

ing God to help you lay these feelings aside and to help you turn your jealousy into love and contentment. As an action step, consider taking on a secret act of service to bless this person in some way.

If you decide to take on a secret act of service for the person you feel jealousy toward, start by praying that your heart would be in it for the right reason. You don't want to serve and feel resentment about it—that doesn't accomplish the purpose of this activity. However, if you can serve them with a heart of openness and love, take note of what grows in your heart toward them. It's very difficult to harbor ill feelings toward a person you are truly serving in love.

Envy: feeling of discontent or covetousness w/ regard to another's success, advantages
Jealous: feeling resentment against someone bc of that person's rivalry, success, or advantages

Pray, "Lord, show me who you want
me to bless today." Then keep your
eyes open for opportunities to bless
others without being noticed.

Day 5
Living into a New Reality

Read Genesis 37:25–36.

The brothers looked up and saw a caravan of Ishmaelites approaching (verse 25). A few verses later they are called Midianite merchants (verse 28). It's possible that they were the same group of people or that they were two groups traveling together. Either way, both of these groups are considered relatives to Joseph and the brothers since they all have the same great-grandfather, Abraham. Abraham bore the Midianites through Keturah (Genesis 25:1–2) and the Ishmaelites through Hagar (verse 12). They are distant relatives, but family nonetheless. As was stated earlier, it was a messy and dysfunctional family history and it had been that way for a few generations.

18. What did Judah propose to the brothers when he saw the caravan? What seems to be his motivation?

Selling him to the Ishmaelites
"let not our hand be upon him, for
he is our brother, our own flesh."

The brothers sold Joseph for twenty shekels, which is about eight ounces, of silver. This is just one more sting that shows how much they despised Joseph. Exodus 21:32 tells us that the normal value for a healthy slave was thirty shekels. The brothers, by taking only two-thirds of the value of a healthy slave, showed how little they valued their brother and how much they wanted to get rid of him.

Also, as an aside, slavery, while discussed in Scripture, is not endorsed by Scripture. In the same way, multiple wives are also discussed yet not encouraged. These two things were happening and, while they weren't and aren't God's best, God wanted to make sure that these vulnerable people were cared for appropriately.

It's also worth noting that Joseph didn't go quietly. Genesis 42:21 tells us that Joseph pleaded with his brothers for his life. I can only imagine the fear and pain in his voice and eyes as he begged his brothers to have mercy.

19. According to Genesis 37:29, which brother wasn't there? What do you think it says about him that he left in the middle of this whole scenario? What was his reaction when he couldn't find Joseph?

> Reuben "and I, where shall I go? – Worried about losing favor w/ his father.

20. The brothers fabricate their alibi and bring Joseph's robe back to their father (verses 31–35). What does Jacob do? Who tries to comfort him? What do you think it was like for the brothers, especially Reuben and Judah, to see their father in this state while harboring their secret?

> Dissonance, guilt.

21. In this chapter, we saw Joseph, Jacob, and the brothers' lives take a drastic turn. In the chart below, write a few words to summarize where each person started at the beginning of this chapter and where they wound up at the end. While we can't know exactly what each person was thinking and feeling, it is helpful for us to pause and consider what these turns of events might have been like for them—remembering that these were real people, and this is a real story. With that in mind, take a few moments to imagine what emotions and thoughts each person or group might have had to contend with. For example, verses 34–35 tell us Jacob was inconsolable in his grief. I've added this for you, but feel free to ponder more of what he could have been thinking and feeling.

	Joseph	Jacob (Israel)	Brothers
Started as	Prideful, ego,	pride in his son, care for his sons	jealous
Ended as	traumatized betrayed	Torn + debilitated devestated	Abusive Conspiring
Emotions to contend with	abandoned sadness	Inconsolable grief	shame hardness of heart

Joseph's life took a harsh and unforeseen turn. When he woke up the morning his dad sent him to check on his brothers, I'm guessing he thought he would go do this task and then head home to let their father know how everything was going. That day probably felt like just another day. But it wasn't. Unfortunately, we've all had these days. Days where unforeseen events or news intersected our lives, like it or not.

22. Think back over your life and choose a moment when you had one of these days when your life took an unexpected turn. What happened? How did this day impact your relationship with God?

Dad getting fired/ lies revealed

23. Read the verses below and circle why you can confidently trust in the Lord even in uncertainty.

    I [Jesus] have told you these things, so that in me you may have peace. In this world you will have trouble. But take heart! I have overcome the world. (John 16:33)

    God has said, "Never will I leave you; never will I forsake you." So we say with confidence, "The Lord is my helper; I will not be afraid. What can mere mortals do to me?" (Hebrews 13:5–6)

24. While we may not be facing a trial that has thrust our life in a totally unexpected direction, we are all facing trials. How do these verses specifically encourage you in a current trial you are facing?

    He is with me. He is ACTIVELY PRESENT and will provide the daily bread necessary.

25. Take a few minutes to pray about this trial, giving it over to
    the Lord and asking him for the peace he promises.

                              ⚹
                            ·······

"If the story of Joseph and the whole of the Bible is true, then
anything that comes into your life is something that, as painful as it is, you need in some way. And anything you pray for
that does not come from him, even if you are sure you cannot
live without it, you do not really need."

                                              —Timothy Keller[2]

                            ·······

PRACTICE REFLECTION

1. Were you able to serve someone in secret this week? If so, what happened?

2. What did you notice about yourself or God as a result of doing this act of service with no one noticing?

Joseph's whole journey started because Jacob favored him over his brothers. This favoritism led to hate and jealousy. And these dark emotions festered and grew as the brothers fed off each other. Small taunts led to small abuses, which led to larger taunts and larger abuses. No one stepped in to stop it. Not Jacob, as a parent, and not Reuben, as the oldest brother. One can only imagine what a family dinner was like with this crew. And then there was Joseph, who, while mostly innocent, did instigate by flaunting dreams and coats. But no amount of immature behavior on his part deserved what ultimately happened to him. Ripped from his family, from his homeland, from everything he knew, and then forced into a life of hard labor. No more choices. Play by someone else's rules or the consequences would be dire.

How does one survive such injustice?

The only way for Joseph to survive was to remember who his God was . . . and to remember the dreams. These dreams, while handled poorly, were a prophetic vision from God. They were a promise to Joseph about his future.

This is how we also survive anything that feels unfair or unjust.

We remember our future. We remember that because of our faith in Jesus, there is a day coming where everything sad will become untrue (to paraphrase J. R. R. Tolkien in *The Return of the King* and Revelation 21:4). And until that day, keep your eyes on Jesus and trust in the truth that he will never leave you or forsake you.

If you don't know if you believe in Jesus, or if you don't have a relationship with him, this is the time to do something about it. Why face another day without the hope he offers? Can I encourage you to explore this with your group leader, a Christian friend, or your pastor?

TURNING FROM TEMPTATION

Day 1
Practice—Memorizing Scripture

There isn't much we have to remember today. We can create lists on our phones, set alerts in our calendars, and use Google to grab pertinent information at a moment's notice. It's liberating in so many ways—especially for us forgetful types. I don't even know my parents' cell phone numbers. I put them in my phone once and never looked at them again. Now I just tell my phone to call them and it does. Amazing.

I can't even imagine living without my smartphone, let alone imagine what it must have been like before the printing press or even earlier than that. If you wanted to remember something important back then, you needed to commit it to memory. This was especially true for Scripture. If you needed an encouraging Bible verse, you had better already know it. The good side of this, of course, is that what we think about and meditate on shapes and forms us.

The downside of living in this smart-technology age is that for many of us, we don't have much, if any, Scripture memorized. We haven't felt the need. Why memorize when you can easily look it up? And while I am thankful for search engines that pull up hundreds of verses at the click of a button, I'm even more thankful for God's words that are stored deep in my heart and soul. These verses are ready when I need them, no matter when or where or if I have access to Wi-Fi. I don't want to give you a false impression of me, though; I don't have tons of verses memorized, but the ones I do come to my rescue often.

Just this week I woke up in the middle of the night and started to feel anxious. It was two in the morning—and we all know nothing good happens at that hour. My brain started churning on all the work I needed to do . . . reach out to that person, finish up the project, follow up with so-and-so . . . you know the drill. And then my thoughts started to jump around. How are my kids, my parents, my friends? And then the what-if scenarios came. I don't know about you, but my thinking can get pretty dark at that time of night. I was spiraling, and I was now wide awake. And then I was worried because I had just made a mental list (that I knew I would forget) of all the really important things I must do as soon as morning dawned, and if I stayed awake much longer I would be unproductive because I would be so tired. The day would be wasted and then the list would just pile up even higher. This whole process took longer for you to read about than it took me to experience. I went from dead asleep to watching my ceiling fan wide-eyed in just minutes. This two o'clock wake-up call has been a pattern for me, and with just a few moments of mental spiraling I can stay awake for hours. I've tried chamomile tea, moving to a new spot, reading a book—if it's been suggested, I promise, I've tried it.

There is one thing that has helped, though: reciting verses of Scripture. On this particular night, Psalm 23 popped into my head, so I went with it. I didn't get much past verse 1: "The LORD is my shepherd, I lack nothing." I said this to myself over and over again. And then I started to ponder what it meant. What does it mean that he is my shepherd—how does that mean he is caring for me? And do I truly believe that I lack nothing? As I recited this one verse, I moved from anxiety to surrender. I started to trust in God as my Good Shepherd who provides for all my needs. I realized that even if I was up all night, I could still trust that he would give me what I needed for the next day. Maybe the day would look different than the list I had just created in my head, but I believed it would be a day the Lord would guide me through and provide for me in. The anxious thoughts still wanted in. They tried to sneak in at all the pauses. I had to redirect my mind at least a hundred times. I didn't fall asleep instantly, but my mind and heart settled. This middle of the night wake-up call actually became a meaningful and sweet time of surrendering to the Lord instead of me becoming an anxiety-riddled mess.

But if I didn't have a verse like Psalm 23:1 already in my mind, that would have never happened. It's not just in the middle of the night that we need to have God's Word stored up. We also need it for those tense conversations, moments when unwelcome news comes, times of temptation or chaos, or quite frankly when anything goes wrong. And on the positive side, we need God's Word so we can encourage a friend when she's struggling and stay encouraged ourselves. Having God's Word memorized helps us remember the truth that we can trust him no matter the scenario.

This week, we are going to memorize Scripture. To do this, choose a verse that is encouraging, meaningful, or speaks to a specific situation you are dealing with. Some ideas, including themes, are:

Psalm 23—part or all, psalm of comfort
Proverbs 3:5–6—trusting in God
Matthew 6:9–13—the Lord's Prayer
John 15:4–5—abiding in God
1 Corinthians 10:13—dealing with temptation
Philippians 4:6–8—anxiety and requests of God

Once you have chosen your passage, write it down and place it where you will see it so you can start committing it to memory. There are lots of tricks to help you memorize. Start by reciting it aloud over and over, then say it without looking at it, and then try writing it down. Some people find it helpful to do memory work at the same time each day—like when you brush your teeth. There are even some Scripture memory apps you can download, or you could set it as the background on your smartphone.

No matter how you do it, the point is to commit the verse to memory so it's ready when you need it. One more tip—to ensure you don't forget what you've memorized, go back and review regularly. Our goal will be to share these verses with our group next week as a way to encourage each other and celebrate our good work.

- Which passage will you recite?

Psalm 23

- Take a moment to write it down and place it where you will see it.

Recitations

- Say a prayer asking God to help you commit this verse to memory this week.

PRACTICE REMINDER

Remember to work on your
Scripture memory passage.

Day 2
Prospering

Read Genesis 39:1–6.

You may have noticed that we skipped over Genesis 38. We did this because, while an important chapter that reveals information about Joseph's brother Judah, it does not contribute to the current story line of Joseph.

Genesis 39 picks up right where chapter 37 left off, with Joseph being taken down to Egypt and bought by Potiphar. Potiphar served the Pharaoh, who was like the king of Egypt, in an official role. It's not entirely clear what his role as "captain of the guard" (verse 1) entailed, but some historical theologians think it's possible that he was the chief executioner. If so, he would have overseen a team of men who executed others on behalf of the Pharaoh. No matter what the details of his role, he was not a man to mess around with.

1. Describe Joseph's new situation. What might have been different about his new life as Potiphar's slave versus his previous life as Jacob's son?

Bought as a slave by Potiphar from the ishmaelites.
~~Joseph~~ The LORD was w/ Joseph.
Joseph was valued + given a lot of responsibility bc the LORD caused Joseph to succeed. Respect?

2. Think of someone you know who you would describe as prospering. Describe them and their life. What do you think it meant that Joseph prospered (verses 2–3)? How does this challenge or expand your idea of what it means to prosper?

Joseph prospered. Sit with that for a moment. He's been sold as a slave. Taken to a foreign land. He had to learn a new language and new customs. He had to adjust to new foods—and that was whatever they fed slaves. He was alone. Everything was different. Everything must have been hard. There had to have been many nights when he wept. Tears of sadness. Tears of grief. Tears of anger. Many nights when he clung to hope that maybe someone would come for him. And then as the days and nights wore on, somewhere along the way, he knew. He knew this was his life. There was no getting out of it. Adjust or die. And it seems Joseph did more than adjust; he embraced his new life and tried to make the most of it.

3. Read Proverbs 3:5–6 and Philippians 4:11–13. How do you see Joseph living according to the principles outlined in these verses?

4. Would you describe your life as prospering right now? Why or why not? Are there any shifts you can make that would help you trust God more in whatever circumstances you are facing?

I think it's important for us to pull away from the world's definition of prosperity. The world tells us we're prospering when our bank account is full, our clothes are designer, and our car is flashy. But this isn't what Scripture teaches. In fact, all we have to do is look to Jesus to see how wrong the world's definition of prosperity is. In Luke 9:58 Jesus states that he "has no place to lay his head." Jesus didn't even have a physical home. He worked a blue-collar job as a carpenter, and he owned very little. But what he did have was worth so much more—he had a deep and abiding relationship with God, and as a result he prospered.

In my life, I've felt the most prosperous when I've been the closest to Jesus. In fact, one of the times I would describe as a time of great prosperity was when we lived in a friend's unfinished basement. We didn't have what the world said we should have but we did have enough, and because of this just-enough provision my faith in the Lord grew. This experience helped me redefine prosperity. I learned that contentment wasn't found in what I did or did not possess, but it was found in my relationship with the Lord. This season of stripping away most of our possessions helped me refocus on what was truly important, and because of this I prospered.

5. What do you think it means that the Lord was <u>with</u> Joseph (verse 2)? Who else noticed that the Lord was with **Potiphar** Joseph (verse 3)? The Egyptians were a polytheistic culture, meaning they worshipped many gods. How do you think Potiphar knew it was the Lord as opposed to another god?

God's presence linked to Joseph's commitment to the Lord!
· Joseph's life in Egypt governed by God's providential care.

12:3. 18:18 to Promises to Patriarchs ?

6. Joseph represented the Lord well through what he did and how he did it. Thinking over your past week, where do you think your actions represented the Lord well? Do you think anyone knew this was because of your faith in God? Why or why not? Is there something you should change or continue as a result of this reflection?

Joseph was given complete trust and complete control over Potiphar's estate. Potiphar concerned himself with nothing except his next meal. Must have been nice for Potiphar. Unfortunately, it didn't just end there. Verse 6 continues with, "Now Joseph was well-built and handsome." Cue the music and the curtain drop. The drama is just about to get started.

PRACTICE REMINDER

Remember to work on your
Scripture memory passage.

Day 3
Standing Strong

Read Genesis 39:6–10.

We aren't really sure how old Joseph was. We do know that he was sold when he was seventeen. Months or years could have passed since then. Here's what we do know: Joseph was still a young man, and a strapping young man at that. It didn't take long for him to get noticed by Potiphar's wife.

7. What is the proposition made to Joseph and how many times does it happen? What is Joseph's response and reasoning? What does Joseph say specifically about this action and what it would mean toward God? What do you think Joseph's response says about his relationship with God?

"Lie w/ me".
Joseph rightly sees that this wd. not only be a sin against his master but against God.

8. According to Ephesians 5:3 and James 4:17, why would sleeping with Potiphar's wife qualify as sin?

Sexual immorality.

9. Joseph refused to go to bed with her. What else did he do to protect himself from this temptation (Genesis 39:10)? How did Joseph show wisdom in setting this boundary?

He did not listen to her + ~~possibly~~ avoided being w/ her.

❊

"Character is not formed instantaneously in moments of pressure; rather, it's in moments of pressure that we discover what's already been formed in our souls."

—Nicole Unice[1]

10. We all face temptations. Think of an area where you tend to struggle (for example, anger, self-control, gossip, envy, lust, anxiety, or overindulgence). What is one specific way you can apply the principle from question 9 to this area of your life? Make a plan to take this action this week.

Slowness to speak.
Put phone away.
Take deep breaths.

11. When we don't succeed in resisting sin, what should we do next (1 John 1:9)? Why can we be assured that we are forgiven (Romans 3:23–24)? How does this truth comfort you?

Confess our sing.

Jesus lived a perfect life without sin. When he died on the cross, he took all the sins of the world upon himself. All of them, including ours. His death paid the full penalty for our sin (Romans 6:23). Our faith in him gives us assurance that we are forgiven. Over and over again. And yet, we also know from experience that sin has very real consequences. An outburst of anger leaves wounded people behind. A quick word of gossip lingers in the heart and creates division and distrust. Joseph knew this truth. Sleeping with Potiphar's wife might have been enjoyable for a moment, but it would have destroyed his trustworthiness and it would have damaged Joseph's witness about the God he served. Ultimately this is what sin does. When we choose our way over God's way, we hurt not only ourselves but also those around us.

And yet, the good news of the gospel is that there is always a way to restoration. We can be restored into an intimate relationship with God by turning back to him and confessing what we have done. This happens the instant we ask. The restoration process for damage to others may take longer, but with God's help it is almost always possible (at least on some level).

PRACTICE REMINDER

Remember to work on your
Scripture memory passage.

Day 4
Resisting Temptation

Read 1 Peter 5:8–9 and Matthew 4:1–11.

12. Read 1 Peter 5:8–9 again, below. Circle who your real enemy is. Underline what he seeks to do to you.

    Be alert and of sober mind. Your enemy the (devil) prowls around like a roaring lion looking for someone to devour. Resist him, standing firm in the faith.

    What are some practical ways you can be alert and sober-minded and stand firm in your faith to resist your enemy? If you have tried some of these tactics in the past, how have they been successful?

Joseph is a great example for how to stand strong and resist the lure of sin. He set boundaries and gave a clear and firm no to his temptress. He isn't the only one who shows us how to stand firm in the presence of our enemy. Jesus also shows us this through his temptation in the wilderness. Let's examine the passage in Matthew to see what other tactics we can learn that can help us resist the enemy.

Temp -> lack of trust in that God's given enough.

(Adam 1
Garden, Abundant food

Adam 2 49 (Jesus)
Desert, w/o food.

13. According to Matthew 4:1–11, who led Jesus into the wilderness and who did the tempting? Why do you think it was important for Jesus to be tempted by the enemy? What else does verse 2 tell us about Jesus's physical state going into this trial? Why do you think this is important?

The Spirit led Jesus into the desert. "to be tempted by the devil."

He was hungry + had fasted for 40 days + nights.

14. Fill in the chart below summarizing the three temptations and Jesus's response.

"Take the Crown before the Cross"

The enemy targets our weakness

Temptation	Response
verse 3 "If you are the Son of God, command these stones to become loaves of bread.	verse 4 "It is written, 'Man shall not live by bread alone, but by every word that comes from the mouth of God."
verses 5–6 If you are the Son of God, throw yourself down, for it is written "He will command his angels concerning you'...	verse 7 Again it is written, You shall not put the LORD your God to the test."
verses 8–9 All these I will give you if you fall down + worship me.	verse 10 Be gone Satan! For it is written, You shall worship the LORD your God + him only you shall serve."

prove yourself

Satan quotes scripture

★ SATAN IS MISUSING SCRIPTURE

Do you actually trust that God will provide what you need?

What do you notice that is similar between each of the three responses? Why do you think the enemy chose these specific temptations? How do Jesus's responses show that he trusted God?

"It is written"

15. When Jesus said, "It is written," it was a signal that he was quoting Old Testament Scripture. Read Psalm 119:11. How do Jesus's responses to the enemy illustrate this truth? Why do you think hiding God's Word in our heart, through memorizing Scripture, helps keep us from sin? Have you experienced this truth in action before? If so, describe what happened and how knowing God's Word helped you choose him over whatever temptation you were facing.

16. Read 1 Corinthians 10:13. Summarize what this verse says about temptation and how we can be strong. How did Jesus illustrate this truth through his actions? How have you seen this truth in your life?

Resisting temptation is never easy, and while your enemy can be relentless, he is never more powerful than our God (1 John 4:4). The truth to remember here is that there is always a way out. You always have a choice. Storing God's Word in your heart is a great tool that will help you stand strong in your faith. The next time you find yourself in a precarious moment, pushed to the brink and tempted to sin, God's Word will be a rescue line. All you have to do is reach out and grab hold of it. And then find the way out that God promises to provide.

The preparation for resisting these future scenarios starts now, though. Time you spend in God's Word, studying and meditating on his truths, and ultimately storing these truths in your heart, is preparation for a future battle with the enemy. These times of preparation are often riddled with the enemy's attempts to distract and derail. He doesn't want you to be prepared. He doesn't want you to know how to fight him successfully. So, the first thing you can do is keep your time in God's Word as a high priority in your life.

Temptations and trials will come, but you can be ready. And you never have to fight alone—God is always ready to help.

PRACTICE REMINDER

Remember to work on your
Scripture memory passage.

Day 5
Running Away

Read Genesis 39:11–20.

Joseph stood firm on his convictions and maintained good
boundaries. It couldn't have been easy, though. Potiphar's wife
was relentless as day after day she threw herself at him. Like our
crafty enemy, she prowled around in persistence and hoped to
wear him down.

17. According to verses 11–12, what happened? What made
    Joseph vulnerable in this particular situation? Now try to
    put yourself in Joseph's shoes for a moment. How do you
    think he felt when she grabbed him? Why do you think he
    chose to run away?

18. Earlier we saw Joseph set good boundaries as a way to
    protect himself from temptation and ultimately sin, and
    now we see him physically and immediately remove him-
    self from the situation. Reflect back on question 10 and
    the place you identified as a struggle. Is it possible to apply
    Joseph's example of fleeing temptation to this area of your

life? If so, how could you do this? Make a plan for how you will implement this the next time you are faced with this temptation.

19. Why do you think Joseph was able to resist this temptation of momentary pleasure? What do you think this says about his trust in God and God's plan for his life, even in difficult circumstances? When you think about your own struggles to give in to temptation, how can trusting God help you resist temptation?

20. What did Potiphar's wife do next (verses 13–18)? Why do you think she did this?

The irony shouldn't be lost on us that Joseph's cloak was used as evidence against him. It echoes the ornate robe of his past that was violently torn from his body and used as evidence to prove his false death. Both of these instances are injustices, and both reveal that Joseph had few choices and little control. Once again, he found his future, and his very life, in the hands of another.

21. When Potiphar heard his wife's story, how did he react and what did he do? If Potiphar was the chief executioner, do you think his reaction was expected? What other action could he have taken instead of jailing Joseph, and why do you think he didn't do this?

22. Have you ever been falsely accused? What happened and how did it make you feel? Did the situation get resolved? If so, how? Where do you think God was in the midst of this situation?

I'll never forget one of the first times I was falsely accused. I was in second grade. I turned my homework in to my teacher, but she couldn't find it. She asked where it was and I insisted I had turned it in. She became increasingly frustrated with me as she asked me over and over to tell her the truth. I told her again and again that I had done what she asked. She didn't believe me and so took me by the arm to the broom closet out in the hallway.

This was back in the day when corporal punishment was acceptable and legal.

I will never forget the flat bristled wooden broom head that she grabbed to spank me with. I was terrified. Tears streamed down my face as she asked me once more to tell her the truth. I almost lied just to avoid being spanked, but right at the perfect moment, there was a knock on the door. She opened it to see another teacher holding out my homework paper and apologizing because she had grabbed it to write a recipe on the back when they were talking a few minutes before this whole incident happened. My teacher gathered me into her arms and apologized profusely.

I honestly don't remember how I felt in that moment, but I do know I was glad I didn't get spanked. This incident still left a mark, though. I will never forget the feeling of knowing I hadn't done anything wrong but not being able to prove my innocence. I was helpless and at the mercy of someone more powerful than I was. It was a terrible feeling.

I can only imagine how Joseph felt. My false accusation would have resulted in the one-time injustice of a spanking. Then I imagine we would have all moved on. But for Joseph, this false accusation would upend his life once again. How does one endure under such a huge injustice? I'm not sure, but based on what we know of his life, I think he turned to the only thing he could— his faith in the Lord. And this faith made Joseph stand strong in his integrity. He resisted temptation and did all the right things. Unfortunately, his accuser didn't have the same integrity.

"Sometimes God chooses to bless us and make us people of integrity in the midst of abominable circumstances, rather than change our circumstances."
—D. A. Carson[2]

This is a hard reality of life sometimes. Doing the right thing doesn't always lead to the results we hope for. Potiphar took swift action and threw Joseph into prison. Potiphar and his men could do whatever they wanted to Joseph, but they could not take away his faith, his integrity, or the fact that God was with him and was using him in the midst of these incredibly painful trials.

PRACTICE REFLECTION

1. Write down the passage you chose to memorize this week; try doing it from memory.

2. Describe your experience with memorizing Scripture this week.

3. How did memorizing the Scripture you chose impact your relationship with God?

FORGOTTEN

Day 1
Practice—A Voice for the Powerless

Joseph was seventeen years old when his life took a hard left turn (Genesis 37:2). Seventeen. He had his whole life ahead of him. His future most likely held marriage, children, and taking over the family business. He had so much to look forward to. And then, just like that, he was sold. Abused, betrayed, and cast out—by those who should have protected him. The future he dreamt of was obliterated with one swift injustice by his brothers. Somehow, he found the strength to lean on God as he cobbled together a new life, making the most of his circumstances. And then he was dealt another blow by Potiphar that landed him in prison.

The only comfort I can find as I contemplate these terrible events for Joseph are these words from Genesis 39:21: "The LORD was with him; he showed him kindness and granted him favor." Read that again, "The LORD was with him." Psalm 34:18 echoes this same truth, "The LORD is close to the brokenhearted and saves those who are crushed in spirit." Joseph's spirit had to be crushed. Mine certainly would have been.

Joseph's story feels extreme. Unbelievable in many ways. Sold by family. Imprisoned for doing the right thing. Forgotten. It's easy to disconnect from the reality of Joseph's story and read it as just that—a story. But it isn't just a story—Joseph was a real person, who suffered real injustice.

What would it be like to be thrown into prison for doing the right thing? Honestly, I hope I never have to find out. I know you hope the same. But there are men and women in prison right now just because they are followers of Jesus—just because they did the right thing by standing strong in their faith. Take Yousef Nadarkhani, for example. He is imprisoned in Iran, separated from his wife and children, serving a six-year prison sentence just for being a follower of Jesus. His stand for Jesus has come at great cost to him and his family. He's been beaten, had his life threatened, and been arrested and imprisoned more than once, even having the death penalty on his head and then rescinded. Yousef, in many ways, is a modern-day Joseph; they even have similar names. Like Joseph, Yousef has very few rights. He is at the mercy of the government and the prison. He is largely forgotten.

Unfortunately, Yousef's story isn't unique. I wish it were. I found his story on the website of PrisonerAlert, a ministry of The Voice of the Martyrs.[1] This ministry, whose mission is to serve persecuted Christians, provides a list of men and women who are in prison because of their faith. This week for our practice I want to invite you to do two things.

First, visit PrisonerAlert online (www.prisoneralert.com) or another website that is similar. You can search "people in prison for faith in Jesus" and you should get some results. Of course, be discerning and do a little digging about where the information is coming from to make sure it is reputable.

Choose someone who is in prison and read their story. Now, pray by name for the person you chose. I suggest you write their name down and place it where you will see it so you can pray in earnest for them every day this week.

Second, take action on their behalf. You can choose to write them a letter or even advocate on their behalf by petitioning an official who can make a difference. At the time of this writing,

The Voice of the Martyrs website provides links with all the information for how to write a letter in the recipient's language and petition officials.

Our goal with this practice is twofold. First, it's to help our hearts realize that Joseph's story in Genesis is real and, in many ways, is still happening. God's people are still being stripped of power, thrown in prison, and forgotten. Yes, God sees them. He has not forgotten them. But many other people have forgotten them.

Which leads to our second purpose in this practice—to let them know they are remembered and prayed for. They may not get the letter you write, but what if they do? Can you imagine the deep, soul-level encouragement it would bring them to know someone somewhere is praying and has not forgotten them? We can ask God to be close to them and lift up their crushed spirit, and he will do it. He says he will, so let's ask boldly and specifically on their behalf.

I pray that as you remember a brother or sister in Christ who is suffering for their faith you will be encouraged to stand stronger in your own faith. Draw courage from both Joseph and the persecuted believers of today that you can not only endure but also trust God in the midst of terrible uncertainty.

- Who will you pray for this week? Write their name and some of the details of their story below.

- How will you advocate for them?

PRACTICE REMINDER

Pray by name for someone who is imprisoned
for their faith in Jesus. Pray specifically that they
would feel the Lord's kindness and be granted
favor in the eyes of those in charge of the prison.

Day 2
Success

Read Genesis 39:20–23.

1. What did the Lord do for Joseph while he was in prison
   (verses 21–23)?

> *"But the Lord was with Joseph + showed him steadfast love + gave him favor in the sight of the keeper of the prison.*

Whatever Joseph did, the Lord made it succeed.

I want to stop right here and tell you that I'm struggling with
the fact that the Lord showed kindness to Joseph when he was
in prison. Why didn't he show him kindness by keeping him out
of prison? Why didn't he show him kindness by having Potiphar
know the truth and stand up for Joseph? And for that matter,
why couldn't he show him kindness by helping him avoid this
whole slavery-in-Egypt debacle in the first place?

I don't fully know the answers to those questions, but here's
what I do know. God is God and we are not. Which means he
holds a vast sum of knowledge and understanding that we don't
and can't. We can try to understand what God is doing, and
sometimes we will catch glimpses to help us understand, but
truthfully, we will probably never really know the whole story.

So, what do we do? We go back to what we know is true. Namely, that God is good, and his plans are the best even when they don't make sense.

Jeremiah 29:11 echoes this truth by stating, "'For I know the plans I have for you,' declares the LORD, 'plans to prosper you and not to harm you, plans to give you hope and a future.'" This verse holds so much promise and assurance. It is a Scripture many, including me, find comfort in when we need encouragement about our future. However, this verse has a much deeper and fuller context than a simple promise for a happy and prosperous future.

The background is that the nation of Israel had been forced into exile because they had wandered away from God. This wasn't some arbitrary punishment; they had been warned time and time again to repent of what they were doing. They didn't and as a result, they wound up in servitude to their enemy, the Babylonians. If we back up to verse 10, it helps us better understand the promise found in verse 11. It says, "When seventy years are completed for Babylon, I will come to you and fulfill my good promise to bring you back to this place." This fuller context helps us see that God was reminding the Israelites that, even while they were in a place they did not want to be, they were not forgotten and he did have good plans for them. Yet they would also still remain in exile for seventy years before these plans happened. And seventy years is a long time.

2. How does Jeremiah 29:11 apply to Joseph's life? What do this verse and Joseph's story so far teach you about God and what it means for him to give you a prosperous future?

※

"Our human ways are based on what seems fair. We firmly believe that when someone does what is right, rewards and blessings result. When someone does what is wrong, there are serious consequences, even punishment. But that's our way, not necessarily God's way."

— Charles Swindoll[2]

· · · · · · ·

3. Think of a hard situation you have come through. How was the Lord with you through that season or circumstance? How did he show you kindness? How did this hard situation shape you and your future, especially your relationship with God? (Keep in mind that we may need a little time and distance from hard circumstances before we can recognize God's presence in them. If you are struggling to see how the Lord was with you or showed you kindness in a particular situation, spend some time praying and asking him to help you. Also, consider thinking of a different situation where you can recognize how his presence was with you.)

Joseph is put in charge again. First it was by Potiphar and now it is by the prison warden.

4. Compare Genesis 39:3 with 39:23. What did both Potiphar and the prison warden notice about Joseph? Do you think the prison warden knew it was the Lord who was giving Joseph success? Practically speaking, what do you think it meant for Joseph to have success in whatever he did while he was in prison?

5. How do you define success? When you look at Joseph's life so far, would you say he'd been successful? Why or why not? How does this concept of God giving success in the midst of hard circumstances challenge the way you define success?

PRACTICE REMINDER

Pray by name for someone who is imprisoned
for their faith in Jesus. Pray specifically that
they would have the capacity to see the
needs of and provide care for those around
them despite their hard circumstances.

Day 3
Noticing

Read Genesis 40:1–7.

Two new characters are introduced to the story in chapter 40: the chief cupbearer, who oversaw and poured the king's drinks, and the chief baker, who made the king's food or oversaw those who made it. Both of these people had direct access to the king and could cause him great harm, even death. Thus, both had to be people who were highly trusted. We aren't told what happened, but Pharaoh became angry with them and threw them into prison, where they met Joseph.

6. According to verse 4, how did Joseph interact with these two men? How do you think Joseph "attended" them?

The passage tells us that after some time these men each had a dream. We don't know what "some time" means. It could have been weeks or months—maybe even longer.

7. What did Joseph notice about these two men the morning after their dreams? What did he ask them? Why do
you think Joseph noticed their change in temperament that
day?

According to the New English Translation Bible, the word translated "dejected" in verse 6 could also be translated as "sick,"
"emaciated," or "depressed."[3] The context is that these two men
did not look good. They were sad and down in a noticeable way.

8. Read Philippians 2:3–4 below. Circle what the verse says
not to do. Underline what to do.

Do nothing out of selfish ambition or vain conceit.
Rather, in humility value others above yourselves, not
looking to your own interests but each of you to the
interests of the others.

What do you think "selfish ambition" and "vain conceit"
mean? What types of things might Joseph, who was in
charge of the prison, have done if he acted with selfish ambition or vain conceit?

9. How did Joseph model humility? How did he model not looking to his own interests but to the interests of others? Considering all he had been through, how do you think he was able to do these things?

10. If you were Joseph, what are some ways you might have been tempted to respond to the cupbearer and the baker?

11. Think through your past week. Where did you respond selfishly or not consider the needs of another? Why was this? Prayerfully reflect on this and ask the Lord to help you come up with a plan to respond differently next time. Write your practical ideas below.

PRACTICE REMINDER

Pray by name for someone who is imprisoned
for their faith in Jesus. Pray specifically that
they would have an opportunity to share their
injustice with someone who would believe
their story and has the power to help them.

Day 4
Dreams

Read Genesis 40:8–19.

Joseph not only took notice that the cupbearer and baker had a
downcast disposition but he took the next step and asked them
what was going on.

12. What were the cupbearer's and baker's responses to Jo-
    seph's question? Do you think they were sad because of the
    dreams or the fact that there was no one to interpret them?

13. How did Joseph respond to their statement? Why do you
    think it's important that Joseph pointed to God as the in-
    terpreter of dreams before he said, "Tell me your dreams"?

Dreams play an important role in Joseph's life. God chose to communicate with Joseph about what would happen in his future through a dream, and God gave Joseph a special ability to interpret dreams. This interpretation gift is how God positioned Joseph to be exactly where he needed to be, which we will explore more in the next lesson. Regarding dreams, God speaking through them wasn't all that uncommon in ancient times. A few notable people God spoke to in dreams were Jacob (Genesis 28:12), Solomon (1 Kings 3:5), the magi or wise men (Matthew 2:12), Joseph, the father of Jesus (Matthew 1:20), and the apostle Paul (Acts 16:9).

Another aspect of God-given dreams is that God usually either made the dreams straightforward and easy to understand—like when he told Joseph, the earthly father of Jesus, not to divorce Mary because the baby Jesus was conceived by the Holy Spirit— or he provided someone who could interpret the dream. The Joseph we are studying was a bit rare in that he not only had a prophetic dream that revealed an aspect of the future but he was also able to interpret dreams.

Does God still speak in dreams today? It's a good question. The answer is both yes and no. God can certainly speak to us in dreams today—he is God, after all, and can do whatever he wants. And there are many encouraging stories of God revealing himself through dreams in other cultures. However, in our Western culture, whether that is God's choice or our aversion, hearing from God through dreams does not appear to be the normative experience for most people.

14. The chief cupbearer told Joseph his dream. What did the dream essentially mean for the cupbearer (verses 12–13)? What did Joseph ask of the cupbearer (verse 14)? Why do you think he asked this?

15. Joseph briefly told the cupbearer his story (verse 15). If you were Joseph, what other details do you think you might have told the cupbearer?

16. If you were the cupbearer, what might you have thought of this man who is in prison and his story claiming innocence? Do you think the fact that Joseph was from a different ethnicity and culture might have played into whether the cupbearer believed him?

It's not entirely clear what the Egyptians thought of the Hebrews, but there are a couple of indicators that lead us to believe they held a bias against them. First, Joseph was bought and sold as a slave. Slavery is an age-old tool used to oppress and degrade entire people groups. Second, Genesis 46:34 tells us that "shepherds are detestable to the Egyptians" and Hebrews were sheepherders. And finally, Genesis 43:32 tells us that "Egyptians could not eat with Hebrews, for that is detestable to Egyptians." This may have just been due to a difference in dietary laws and regulations, but to say something is detestable about one group of people to another group of people is a strong indicator that there was some form of prejudice toward them. It's hard to say if this played into what the cupbearer thought and what he did upon his release, but it's also hard to ignore that this may have been a part of why he made the choices he did.

17. When you hear stories, either personally or in the news, of people who are suffering some form of injustice, what makes you tend to believe their story? What makes you tend to distrust their story? Honestly evaluate if race, ethnicity, education, and other similar factors play a role in this. Based on this, if you were the Egyptian cupbearer, do you think you would believe Joseph's story? Why or why not?

The chief baker, when he saw the cupbearer receive a positive interpretation, told Joseph his dream too. Unfortunately, his interpretation wasn't favorable, and Joseph told him that he would soon be executed. The death Joseph describes is particularly gruesome and devastating for an Egyptian because they believed that the preservation of the body was somehow linked to the afterlife (hence all the Egyptian mummies). Joseph's interpretation essentially destroys all hope for the baker. He would not only die but his perceived chance at an afterlife would also be taken away when the birds ate his body.

18. What do you imagine Joseph, the cupbearer, and the baker each thought about and felt over the next three days while they were waiting?

Joseph

Cupbearer

Baker

We've all heard the old adage, "Life isn't fair." The baker and cupbearer are a prime example of this. Why is it some people have lives deeply marked by pain and suffering, while others seem to get a relatively easy and carefree life? I don't have an answer, and I think it is futile to try to come up with one. Instead, we should resolve to keep our eyes on God and remember what is true, instead of comparing our lives to others'. If you are in a season of pain, the truth is, God sees you, loves you, and has not forgotten you. If you are in a season of ease, God sees you, loves you, and has not forgotten you either. No matter what your life seems to be marked by, remember that God is good and he wastes nothing. You can trust him.

• • • • • • •

PRACTICE REMINDER

Pray by name for someone who is imprisoned
for their faith in Jesus. Pray specifically that
they would hear news this week that would
help them know they have not been forgotten.

Day 5
Forgotten

Read Genesis 40:20–23.

19. What happened after three days? How did this align with Joseph's interpretation of the cupbearer's and baker's dreams?

20. It's presumable that Joseph heard what happened to the cupbearer and baker. How do you think it felt to Joseph to know that he was able to accurately interpret dreams? Reflect back to the beginning of Joseph's story (Genesis 37:5–7, 9–10). How could knowing these interpretations were accurate have encouraged him regarding the dreams he had years ago?

21. What do you think Joseph hoped would happen once the cupbearer was freed? How do you think Joseph felt as time moved on? Write next to each time marker how you think he was feeling and what he might have been thinking. Remember that Joseph wasn't privy to knowing what we know in verse 23. He was wondering and waiting in real time.

First few days

First few weeks

A few months

Many months

As time moved on, it became evident that Joseph had been forgotten. Knowing what you know of Joseph, what do you think he clung to in these days and months of waiting? How do you think this situation tested or strengthened his trust in God?

22. Why do you think the cupbearer forgot Joseph?

23. We all know what it feels like to be overlooked and forgotten. However, for us, being forgotten doesn't usually mean we are left to languish in prison for years. But the feelings elicited by rejection are deep and real. When was a moment that you felt forgotten by another person or group? How did you handle this and where did you find hope in the midst of this painful season?

24. When you reflect on the above feelings of being overlooked and forgotten, how did they impact your trust in God? What are some practical ways you can choose to trust God the next time something like this happens?

25. It's also true that we, like the cupbearer, are sometimes the ones who forget. Take a moment to prayerfully ask the Lord if there is someone he wants you to encourage today by letting them know you are thinking of them. This could be a friend, coworker, pastor, or missionary. When a name comes to mind, jot it down and then take a few minutes right now to encourage them. You could send a text, write a letter, make a phone call, or make any other creative contact you can think of. What happened as a result of your effort to let someone know you were thinking about them?

I struggle to imagine what this was like for Joseph. Once again, he was left to wait. And wait. And wait. Genesis 41:1 tells us two full years pass. Two years.

Think for a moment: What were you doing two years ago? Imagine if you had just been sitting in prison from that moment until now. It would feel like wasted time, wouldn't it? And yet, in God's economy, no time is wasted. God most certainly used that time to grow and shape Joseph so he would be ready for what was coming.

"This is what the past is for! Every experience God gives us, every person He puts in our lives is the perfect preparation for a future that only He can see."

—Corrie ten Boom[4]

Hebrews 12:10–11 says it this way, "God disciplines us for our good, in order that we may share in his holiness. No discipline seems pleasant at the time, but painful. Later on, however, it produces a harvest of righteousness and peace for those who have been trained by it." Discipline is a growing process that God uses for our good; it is not punishment for something we have done but a way to prepare us for what is coming. God was certainly preparing Joseph for a large harvest of righteousness.

Do you feel sidelined? Does the time feel wasted? Know that you have not been forgotten. Rather, you are being prepared. Keep trusting in God to lead and guide. He will move at just the right moment.

PRACTICE REFLECTION

1. Who did you pray for this week? What about their story resonated with you?

2. How did you advocate for them?

3. What did you learn about yourself and/or God as a result of doing this practice?

REMEMBERED AND RESTORED

DAY 1

Practice—Giving out of Abundance

Finally, something good happened to Joseph. We've read about so many setbacks and downturns for him that I know we are all ready for some good news. The change happened really fast too. One moment he was sitting in prison and the next he was sitting in the palace. With just a few swift decisions by Pharaoh, Joseph was not only removed from a life of destitution but also given a hopeful future. People with power get to do things like that. They get to make an impact, for good or bad. And Joseph had been at the mercy of powerful people for nearly half his life. Finally, a decision fell in his favor.

While Joseph was on this waiting and wondering journey, one thing remained true—God was with him and for him. As we've read, God showed him kindness and granted him favor. He gave him success in everything he did. Joseph seemed to be aware that God was faithfully with him because, incredibly, Joseph also remained faithful to God. When he had an opportunity to take credit for something, he pointed to God instead (Genesis 40:8;

41:16). When he had an opportunity to take pleasure in something that wasn't his, Potiphar's wife, he ran the other direction (Genesis 39:9, 13). He trusted God and remained faithful to God at great cost to himself. But the cost of being unfaithful would have been higher; it always is. Joseph knew that.

In this lesson, we see that Joseph finally got to reap some reward for his faithful endurance. He was just where he needed to be at the exact time he was needed. And because he endured, he was able to use his God-given gifts and skills to save not only himself but also the nation of Egypt, the children Israel, and their neighbors. Hard times were coming and Joseph, by God's sovereignty and grace, was the one who would save them.

I don't want to give too much of the story away, because I want you to read it and discover it for yourself, but one of the parts of this lesson is God revealing that there would be a time of abundance followed by a time of famine. Joseph helped the people save during abundance, so they were ready for the famine. We also have seasons of abundance where we have more than we need and seasons of famine where we find ourselves in need.

One season of need for me was when my husband and I were still newish to marriage and had our first daughter. He was in graduate school, and I was working an hourly job that barely covered our bills, let alone the childcare costs. We were stressed and stretched beyond our capacity. No one in the family was functioning well—I think I cried more than our infant. It was in this place that some dear friends took notice and stepped in.

They evaluated and prayed about what they could do and decided to make the extravagant offer for us to move into their basement. It was a resource they had. They didn't have a lot of money, but they did have some extra space. It wasn't my dream home, nor was it their ideal situation. But they believed God was asking them to take this leap of faith to help us and so they did. God turned their faithfulness into a situation of great abundance for us all. He took our deep friendship to a whole new level. And he taught us that we all had something to offer. They offered their home. And once my tears dried up, I discovered I had places of abundance in my life that I could offer back to them, like helping with meals and their new baby. None of us had large bank accounts, but we all had something to share or give.

Not everyone is called to open their home to others, but we all have something to offer. We all have places of abundance in our lives that we can share to help meet needs. This week for our practice, I want to invite you to prayerfully reflect on places where you have abundance. It could be money, time, a resource, an ability, or something else. Even if you feel stretched thin, we all have something to offer. Jot down some ideas that come to mind. Then prayerfully think about how you could use this area of abundance from your life to help meet a need for someone else. Be creative. It might be sharing a meal, paying for groceries, helping fix a leaking faucet, taking care of your friend's kids, writing a note to someone who can't get out—the ideas are endless.

Pray and see what the Lord brings to mind. And then, most importantly, take action. I'm thankful my friends took action when we were in need. They changed my life. They changed my family's life. I think we changed theirs too. You never know how God will lead you, in little or big ways. God has given you abundance somewhere in your life that will be a blessing to someone in need.

- What are some areas of abundance in my life?

Time w/ my kids, discipleship opportunities

Empathy for exhausted moms. Experience w/ my own baby troubles.

- What are some ideas for how I can use those areas of abundance to help someone in need?

Sending meals, listening, praying, empathizing.

- My plan for how I can share my abundance with someone this week is:

Sending Reyes a meal.

PRACTICE REMINDER

Remember to use an area of abundance
in your life to meet a need around you.

Day 2
Waiting

Read Genesis 41:1.

Genesis 41:1 tells us that two full years passed after Joseph inter-
preted the dreams for the cupbearer and the baker. That means
Joseph spent two entire years sitting and waiting in prison—and
that is after he had already been in prison for some time. What
does one do in an ancient prison for more than two years? While
we don't know for sure what he did, we have a few clues that can
help us understand what it might have been like.

First, we know there was some kind of work for him to do,
since the prison warden put Joseph in charge of all the other pris-
oners (Genesis 39:22). This tells us that while he may have had to
wait two years, he didn't just sit around. He was actively engaged
and seemed to make the most of the situation by doing good work.

Second, we can assume Joseph didn't like his accommodations
very much. In Genesis 40:15, when Joseph made his bold ask that
the cupbearer remember him, he stated, "I have done nothing to
deserve being put in a dungeon." A dungeon. I've never been in
an ancient Egyptian dungeon, but I imagine it to be dark, musty,
and dirty—with probably a few critters I would never want to
sleep with. Now perhaps Joseph was just being hyperbolic in
his description because he was desperate to get out of there, but
either way we can be certain this was no Hilton and there was
definitely no room service. So, while we don't know exactly what
these two years were like for him, it's safe to assume they were
long and difficult years.

1. Joseph was stuck in prison and at the mercy of those who were in power. What kind of prayers do you think he prayed during these two years of waiting? Do you think they changed over time? If so, how? If you were Joseph, what kinds of things would you have asked for?

Possibly prayers for change in circumstance to a change in heart/ strength.

We don't know what Joseph talked to God about during this time, but I'm assuming he asked for many things that didn't happen. God seemed to say no to his prayers—or at the very least he seemed slow in answering the requests. This makes me think of Jesus and his final moments on earth. He knows he is approaching a brutal death at the hands of his enemies, and feeling overwhelmed by this reality he prays, "My Father, if it is possible, may this cup be taken from me. Yet not as I will, but as you will" (Matthew 26:39). Jesus boldly asks God to please find another way. And God says no. God's good and perfect will was that Jesus would endure this terrible death for a much higher purpose—our salvation.

Jesus models a beautiful surrender to God as he makes his bold request but then submits himself to God's will ahead of his own. We often don't get to know why God seems to say no to some of our prayers, but we can trust that he is ultimately working out all things for our good and his glory (Romans 8:28).

2. Why do you think God didn't answer some of these prayers and requests from Joseph?

Bc of the length of time he was in prison.

Joseph's waiting was actually much longer that two-plus years. He was seventeen when he was sold and, in this chapter, we learn that he is now thirty (Genesis 41:46). That means he's essentially been in a season of waiting for thirteen years. Keep in mind that he lived these days in real time. I know that sounds obvious, but when two full years are encapsulated with just a few brief words, it's easy to breeze by the statement without realizing what that really meant for him. For two full years he waited. Counting the days by sunrise and sunset. He had no idea what could become of his life or if he would ever get out of prison. I think he clung to the dreams God gave him (Genesis 37:5–11) as a source of hope, but even then he had to know that God could somehow accomplish this dream without Joseph ever leaving prison.

> ❋
>
> "God will either give us what we ask or give us what we would have asked if we knew everything he knew."
> —Timothy Keller[1]

3. How do you think Joseph was able to keep going day after day during those thirteen years? Thinking back over what we have studied so far, where do you think he found strength and hope to trust God and face each new day? What are some practical things Joseph might have done to help him trust God during this time?

God made the things he did prosper.

4. Think of a few situations that you have had to wait through in the past but that are now resolved. For example: test results, a loved one to turn back to God, an illness, job loss, having a child. Fill in the chart on the next page, keeping in mind that sometimes we don't get to know why God had us wait or why he answered our prayers the way he did. It's OK to say you don't know.

What I waited for	How long I waited	What I prayed for	Why I think God answered how and when he did
Carly to change (still) relief @ home	10 years	How to change	Because it wasn't about her changing. I have tremendously changed + grown as a result of it. (learning to love people for who they are)

5. Looking back, how did the seasons of waiting you listed in the last question impact your relationship with God? If things didn't turn out as you'd hoped, have you been able to move through those situations? If yes, how? If not, why?

6. Now consider some of the ways you are currently waiting.
   It might be a decision to be made, a health crisis, a loved
   one's poor choices, a desired life change, a deep longing
   you have, and so many others. Fill in the chart below regarding these areas of your life.

What I'm waiting for	How long I've been waiting	What I'm praying for	Why I think God hasn't answered yet
Wisdom for school for kids	1 year	Wisdom / clarity / a plan	Because He wants me to trust Him + walk faithfully in what's before me.
church stuff	6 mo - 1 yr.	wisdom, structure, change	learning to press in + have hard conversations.

7. How does thinking about Joseph and your own resolved
seasons of waiting help you as you currently wait?

*It helps to know God is @
work. Our waiting is not
wasted.*

Refining.

As you ponder the question about why God hasn't answered a
prayer yet, keep in mind this truth: God is not withholding something from you to be vindictive or to
try to make you pay him back for
something you did. That is not our
God. That may be how the world
operates at times, but our God is
a God of forgiveness and grace
(Psalm 103:10–12; 1 John 1:9). If
you are waiting for an answer from
the Lord, know you can trust that
he loves you and he is ultimately
working all things for your good
(Romans 8:28).

"But do not forget this one
thing, dear friends: With the
Lord a day is like a thousand
years, and a thousand years
are like a day. The Lord is not
slow in keeping his promise,
as some understand slowness.
Instead he is patient with you,
not wanting anyone to perish, but everyone to come to
repentance."

—2 Peter 3:8–9

PRACTICE REMINDER

Remember to use an area of abundance
in your life to meet a need around you.

Day 3
Remembered and Released

Read Genesis 41:1–32.

8. Write or draw out Pharaoh's two dreams found in verses
   1–7. According to verse 8, how did these dreams impact
   Pharaoh and what did he do about it? Why do you think
   these dreams were so troubling to Pharaoh?

The cupbearer, witnessing some or all of this, suddenly had his
memory triggered and remembered Joseph. He then told Pharaoh
about Joseph's ability to interpret dreams.

9. According to verse 14, what happened to Joseph? Imagine for a minute what this might have been like. What do
   you think Joseph might have been thinking or feeling when
   he heard someone enter the prison? What about when he

heard his name called as the one they were looking for? What about when he heard who needed him?

SEEN

Joseph took a few minutes to shave and change clothes, and presumably bathe, before he saw Pharaoh. While this may seem like a sidebar detail that doesn't further the story, it actually highlights once again that Joseph was in a totally new culture. Egyptians tended to be clean-shaven and Hebrews tended to wear beards. I'm not sure if Joseph was told to shave or if he asked to shave. Either way, he did so—and it seems he did so willingly. He knew he was going before the king and he would have one opportunity to make an impression. The king held absolute power over what would be next for Joseph, whether it was a death sentence, a release, or something else.

10. According to verse 15, what did Pharaoh tell Joseph he had heard about him? Imagine this situation: If you were Joseph, what might have been some of your hopes and fears in this moment? How did Joseph respond in verse 16? What do you think this response says about Joseph's trust in God?

"I have heard ... when you hear a dream you can interpret it." I bet he wrestled w/ wanting to sell himself/abilities + giving God the credit.

This moment in Joseph's life amazes me. Joseph had been through so much and here was an opportunity to impress the king. If it were me, I would have been so tempted to try to make myself look good. "Yes, in fact I can do this. I can interpret dreams. I am very skilled at this work you need done." I think I would be peacocking all over the place: "Look at me, look at me, look at me. I have what you need. And if I can do this for you, just think of how valuable I could be to your future." But this isn't what Joseph does. He points to God instead. He says, "I cannot do it, but God will."

Joseph trusted God. In the midst of such uncertainty, Joseph didn't even blink. He showed an implicit trust in God and his sovereign control over his life and his future.

11. Read verses 25–32 again and count the number of times *God* is used. Considering the fact that Egyptians did not traditionally worship the one true God, but many gods, why do you think God chose to reveal the coming abundance and famine to Pharaoh?

> To show that He is the
> one TRUE God.
> He is over all things.

12. Summarize what Joseph said the two dreams meant. Why did God give two dreams? When would all of this take place? According to verse 32, who does Joseph say has decided this will happen and who is responsible for doing it? What do you think this says about God and his involvement in both good and hard times?

> It is fixed by God +
> He will shortly bring
> it about.

13. Reflecting on Joseph's life and your own life, why do you think God allows hard things to happen? Have you had a hard experience that ultimately turned out for your good or the good of those around you? What happened?

Hard situations grow our trust and dependence on God.

"In this world you will have trouble, but take heart, I have overcome the world."

Remember to use an area of abundance
in your life to meet a need around you.

Day 4
Restored

Read Genesis 41:33–45.

Joseph told Pharaoh exactly what God was going to do. There
would be seven years of abundance followed by seven years of
severe famine. The famine would be so severe that if they did not
start preparing right away, the consequences would be dire.

14. According to verses 33–36, what did Joseph tell Pharaoh
    should be done next? Did Pharaoh ask for this recommen-
    dation? Why do you think Joseph gave this advice?

> To hire a wise + discerning man.
> Maybe b/c Joseph knew he could
> do it.

This is another interesting moment in Joseph's life. A few verses
ago, when he had the opportunity to take credit for his ability to
interpret dreams, he pointed to God instead. In this moment, we
see him offer unsolicited advice. Is he trying to take control of the
situation and prove his worth? Maybe. However, based on what
we have seen of Joseph's life so far, it is more likely that either he
saw this as a God-given opportunity and he spoke truth into it,
or the Lord instructed Joseph to share and we just aren't privy to
that detail. Pharaoh could listen or not, that was his choice, but
Joseph would go to bed that night knowing he did what he could.

15. Is there any area in your life where you might need to speak up to offer your thoughts and wisdom about what you see happening around you? If something comes to mind, take some time to prayerfully consider how you could do this. Take a few minutes to journal and pray about this. Specifically ask the Lord if he is really inviting you to boldly state something or if it's perhaps just something you want to do.

If you feel God is inviting you to take a next step and speak the truth in love to someone, I encourage you to proceed with a posture of openhanded humility. We all know what it feels like to get unsolicited advice from others. If done at the wrong time or with the wrong intentions, not only will it not be heard but it could do damage to a relationship. On the other hand, if God does seem to be asking you to move forward, do so entrusting the results to him. If you are unsure if you should speak up, invite a trusted and wise Christian to help you pray about what the next step should be.

16. Joseph's plan seemed good to Pharaoh. What did he then ask the officials around him (verse 38)? What was ultimately decided and why?

Can we find a man like this in whom is the spirit of God?

A couple of quick notes about Pharaoh's question, "Can we find anyone like this man, one in whom is the spirit of God?" First, what did Pharaoh mean by asking, "Can we find anyone like this man?" It is possible that Pharaoh was asking if they could find anyone like Joseph, but it seems more likely that he meant, "Can we find anyone like the man Joseph just described?" Second, when Pharaoh said he was looking for someone in "whom is the spirit of God," at first glance it seems like he is talking about the one true God, the God of the Hebrews. But I don't think this is the case. While the original Hebrew could be translated as "God," it can also be translated as "gods." Based on what we know of ancient Egypt, it doesn't seem likely that Pharaoh would exclusively seek someone who was indwelt by the Spirit of the one true God. He most likely worshipped many gods and thus it's more likely that he was really saying "one in whom is the spirit of the gods."

Of course, all the other gods are false except the one true God whom Joseph knew. Joseph kept pointing to God as the source of his wisdom and ability—and the one who would enact all that was about to happen.

With this, Joseph received a huge promotion. He was moved from enslaved prisoner to honored dignitary.

17. List all the things Pharaoh did to give Joseph honor with his new role (verses 41–45). Thinking back over all that Joseph had lost over the last thirteen years, how did these things restore what could have been for Joseph if his brothers had never sold him as a slave?

The signet ring is essentially the king's signature. It meant that Joseph had the authority to make any decision on behalf of Pharaoh. The ring gave him final and ultimate say.

18. Thinking about the signet ring and what it meant for Joseph, what surprises you about the fact that Pharaoh gave this ring to him? Why do you think Pharaoh trusted Joseph so implicitly?

19. Has there ever been a time when you were granted trust before you proved you were worthy of this trust? If so, what happened? Why do you think you were trusted in this way? How did it make you feel to know you were trusted?

20. What makes someone worthy of trust? Who are some of the people in your life that you trust implicitly? Why do you trust them? Take a few minutes to thank God for these relationships. Then take a moment right now to send a text or a note to one of these people to express your gratitude for their relationship.

PRACTICE REMINDER

Remember to use an area of abundance
in your life to meet a need around you.

Day 5
Abundance

Read Genesis 41:46–57.

21. During the years of abundance, Joseph and his new wife, Asenath, also experienced abundance by having two boys (verses 50–52). What did he name the boys and what does this say about how Joseph dealt with his past as well as how he was moving forward in his new life?

There's a hope-filled verse in the book of Joel that reveals God's heart for restoration. Joel was an Old Testament prophet who foretold a massive locust invasion that would destroy nearly everything in sight. The prophecy was given to warn God's people and call them to repentance. However, near the end of Joel's hard message of destruction, he also shared an abundant promise of God. He stated that God "will restore to you the years that the swarming locust has eaten" (2:25 ESV).

This verse makes me think of where Joseph was in his life. He had lost so much, and that was never truly replaced. Those thirteen years were like years that swarming locust destroyed. And yet, God restored so much to Joseph's life. God gave Joseph a position of influence that wound up saving many lives. He blessed him with a new family. He blessed him with meaningful work.

What I love about this verse and how it applies to Joseph's life is that it reveals the heart of our God. Our God is in the business of restoration. He started his restoration project the moment sin entered the picture in Genesis 3. Each step of the way since that moment he has been setting up restoration for his people to live into the full and abundant life he always intended us to have. It started with Jesus and his death and resurrection for our sins, and it ends, or rather starts again, when Jesus returns and sets all things right forever. There will be no more tears, no more pain, and no more loss (Revelation 21:1–4). While we aren't promised a restoration here and now for all our broken circumstances, God often does restorative work in our lives. And even if this restoration doesn't look like what we hoped for, we can be certain that there is a day coming when everything will be fully and finally restored.

"Joseph didn't turn his attention to being fruitful only after the season of suffering was over. In the land of his affliction, in the middle of the struggle, in the heart of darkness, Joseph was confident that God was at work."

—Nancy Guthrie[2]

22. Have you ever experienced God's restoration in your life in a way that you might be able to say that God restored the years the locust had eaten? If so, what happened? Did this experience increase your trust in God, and if so, how might it impact the next time you enter into a hard season?

23. Who was impacted by the famine (verse 54)? What did Egypt wind up doing for its neighbors (verse 57)? Why do you think it is significant that the Egyptians shared their abundance with others?

24. When have you been in a season of abundance and had more than you needed? What are some things you did or wish you did to help you prepare for a season of want or need? If you are in a season of abundance now, how can you not only prepare for the future but also share in the present? Are there any changes you feel led to make?

25. As the famine got underway, do you think Joseph understood the real reason God had placed him in Egypt? Why or why not?

Joseph helped the Egyptians save so much grain that they became somewhat humanitarian in their response toward others. When starving and desperate people came into Egypt, the Egyptians sold some of their supply. They made the other people pay, of course—they weren't *that* benevolent.

As Joseph gave out portions of grain, I wonder if he had moments when he thought of his Hebrew family and what had happened to them. Were they starving? Did they need food? Were they even alive? And what of that dream he'd had as a seventeen-year-old? Is this how it would come to pass?

Joseph was about to find out the answers to all these questions.

PRACTICE REFLECTION

1. Over the past few days, how did you share from an area of current abundance in your life with someone in need? What happened?

2. What did you learn about God or yourself as a result of this practice?

THE WEIGHT OF SIN

DAY 1
Practice—Lament

While there's a lot of redemption in the story of Joseph, there is also an incredible amount of sadness and loss. Sin, as it ripples out, has a way of creating more damage than we ever thought possible.

In this instance, it wasn't just Joseph who had to live through the unthinkable because of his brothers' sins; his father was also deeply impacted. In fact, as we will read, it seems Jacob never fully came out of his grief. And then there was Benjamin, Joseph's younger brother. While we don't know much about him, it seems Jacob transferred the mantle of favorite son to him. Imagine what it might have been like to be Benjamin. I'm guessing he carried the weight of trying to ease his father's pain while simultaneously feeling suffocated under his overprotective care. What does that do to a person? And finally, there were the ten brothers who were responsible for this atrocity. They sinned once by harboring hate for Joseph. And again when they sold him. And again when they lied. And again when they chose solidarity to never tell the real story. And again . . . and again . . . and again. They sinned against God, their family, and their community. Imagine the weight of carrying this burden as they witnessed the pain of their father and the rift they created in their family.

We don't know all the details of how each of these people processed the sin and its implications, but we can extrapolate from our own experiences that it wasn't easy for any of them. Hopefully we don't know anything near the depths of what this family had to live through, but we all know what it feels like to lie and be lied to. To reject and be rejected. To gossip and be gossiped against. We know what it feels like to be impacted by sin. It is a heavy weight to bear.

The text does give us a few clues about Joseph and how he processed the injustice done to him. When Joseph's brothers came to Egypt in need, they unknowingly met with Joseph. While they didn't recognize Joseph, he certainly knew who they were. Eventually Joseph, overcome with emotion, had to excuse himself from the conversation to have a private moment to weep. This happened three times before he revealed his true identity. Joseph held the deep pain of their choices in his heart. It's hard to say what emotions were expressed through his weeping—sadness, grief, anger, confusion? Probably a mix of all of these. While we don't know exactly, it is safe to assume that Joseph was in the process of lament, as lamenting holds all of these emotions.

Lamenting is an important practice in Scripture. There's a whole book called Lamentations and nearly a third of the Psalms are considered songs or poems of lament. Lament isn't just an emotional outburst aimed at God to complain or fret; it's a deeper level of sharing and grieving with God as we recognize the brokenness and pain around us and in our own lives. In Scripture, we see lament happen around three primary areas: personal pain, national tragedy, and rampant injustice. Joseph could lament all three.

The lament process laid out in the Psalms generally falls into three movements: protest, petition, and praise. In the protest movement of lament, we freely cry out to God, expressing our raw and real emotions regarding what is broken. In the petition movement, we plead with God to do something about the situation, and we ask him how we should be a part of moving forward. And, finally, in the praise movement, we turn back to God in trust to declare what we know is true of his character.

Psalm 13 is an excellent example of lament. As you read it below, identify the three movements by underlining the verses that express protest, circling the petition, and putting a square around the praise verses.

How long, LORD? Will you forget me forever?
　How long will you hide your face from me?
How long must I wrestle with my thoughts
　and day after day have sorrow in my heart?
How long will my enemy triumph over me?

Look on me and answer, LORD my God.
　Give light to my eyes, or I will sleep in death,
and my enemy will say, "I have overcome him,"
　and my foes will rejoice when I fall.

But I trust in your unfailing love;
　my heart rejoices in your salvation.
I will sing the LORD's praise,
　for he has been good to me.

This week, I want to invite you into the process of lament using the structure of protest, petition, and praise. Like Joseph, we can all lament around personal pain, national tragedy, and rampant injustice. This lamenting process may be new to you, and as with anything new, it may take some getting used to. If you are currently experiencing personal pain, I want to encourage you to start there. Once you've done that, then you can take some time to lament the brokenness you see around you. Lamenting beyond our needs and pain may feel foreign for some of us, but it is a biblical practice as it helps us live out God's exhortation that we be one body with many parts, and when one part suffers, we all suffer (1 Corinthians 12:26).

As we lament broken systems and structures around us, may we take the posture of unity and recognize that when someone else

❋

"Lament is a cry of belief in a good God, a God who has His ear to our hearts, a God who transfigures the ugly into beauty. *Complaint* is the bitter howl of unbelief in any benevolent God in this moment, a distrust in the love-beat of the Father's heart."

—Ann Voskamp[1]

....

suffers, we ultimately suffer too. As we lament, I also encourage you to ask the Lord what you may be called to do about these broken places. Take a few moments to listen to what God may be prompting you to do—you may be called to be a part of the solution.

Each day this week, I will invite you to consider one of these areas to lament. I encourage you to write out your prayers of lament each day—kind of like your own psalms. Today, take some time to brainstorm what areas you could lament and then, in the spaces below, write out your first lament on your personal pain or whichever one you feel most drawn to. You can come back to the other ideas as we move through the lesson this week.

Ideas for Lament

Personal Pain

> *My Parents*
> *Reeni's parents*

National Tragedy

> ~~*Racism*~~
> ~~*Political division*~~
> *Natural disasters.*
> *Ukraine + Russia*

Rampant Injustice

> · *Racism*
> · *Sex trafficing*
> · *Child abuse*

My Lament

Protest

Petition

Praise

PRACTICE REMINDER

Before you start the lesson, take a few minutes
to write a prayer of lament for one of the
areas you identified in the practice section.

Day 2
The Shock of a Lifetime

Read Genesis 42:1–13.

1. According to verses 1–5, what was happening in Canaan
   and what did Jacob do about it? Why did he keep Benjamin
   at home?

   Famine. Sent sons to get food in Egypt.
   "He feared that harm might happen to him."

2. Joseph immediately recognized his brothers. Drawing from
   what we have studied so far as well as how much time has
   passed, why do you think Joseph was not recognizable to
   them (if you need ideas, see 41:14, 42; and also 42:23)?

   Shaved his beard, time, clothing, age

Imagine this moment. It's been more than twenty years since
Joseph had seen his family of origin. He's living a new life with a
new family in a new culture. This moment feels a little like one of
those seedy daytime talk shows where an estranged or long-lost

family member bounds out from backstage, shocking everyone in the audience and nearly sending the unsuspecting family member into cardiac arrest. It's the shock of a lifetime.

In some ways, though, I suspect Joseph knew this day might come. He knew the famine stretched to his family's homeland and so perhaps he had an inclination that they might come to ask for food. And yet when that day arrived, I imagine he was totally shocked to be staring into his brothers' eyes.

3. Think of a moment when you were totally caught off guard, for good or bad, by someone or some news. What happened? In that moment, what did you do and how did you respond? Do you wish you had done anything differently?

4. While we can't really know what was racing through Joseph's heart and mind in this moment, we can empathize with being caught off guard. Joseph initially "pretended to be a stranger and spoke harshly to them" (verse 7). Why do you think he responded like this? If you had been in this situation, what might you have done? Would you be tempted to reveal who you really were? Why or why not?

5. Read and review the original dreams in Genesis 37:6–9. How did Joseph's dreams come to fruition, at least partially, in this moment? Why do you think Joseph remembered the dreams but then accused his brothers of being spies?

It seems a little odd that Joseph accused his brothers of being spies. Why would he do this? There aren't clear answers. However, this was the first in a series of tests that Joseph put his brothers through. It seems these tests were intended to help Joseph know a little more about who his brothers had become over the years. Were they the same type of people who threw him in the cistern and sold him as a slave? Or had they grown and changed for the better?

••••••

The brothers insisted that they were not spies but honest men. Joseph accused them again and finally, in what appears to be an effort to prove their honesty, they told Joseph about their family.

6. What did Joseph learn about the rest of his family in this moment? How do you think it felt for Joseph to know about Jacob and Benjamin? What do you think it felt like for Joseph to hear the brothers refer to him as being "no more" (verse 13)?

PRACTICE REMINDER

Before you start the lesson, take a few minutes
to write a prayer of lament for one of the
areas you identified in the practice section.

Day 3
Testing

Read Genesis 42:14–28.

Joseph heard that his father and youngest brother were alive and
so he formulated a plan to ensure he would see Benjamin.

7. What test did Joseph propose to prove that the brothers
   weren't spies (verses 15–16)? Why do you think seeing Benjamin is so important to Joseph? What could it tell him
   about the brothers and who they had become over the past
   twenty years?

Joseph stated that he would hold everyone and send only one
brother back to get Benjamin. He then threw them all in prison
for three days, possibly the very same prison he spent time in.
After three days, Joseph released the brothers and modified his
proposal.

8. According to verses 18–20, what did Joseph decide to do instead and what was the reason he gave for this change? Why do you think he ultimately chose this course of action instead of his original plan (consider Jacob, the desperate need the family had for food, and any other reasons you think he might have done this)?

Thinking that Joseph couldn't understand them because he had originally used an interpreter, the brothers revealed something very important in this moment—they had been carrying the weight of their guilt for years. It was fresh in their minds. And it appeared they had been continuously looking over their shoulders, waiting for some form of punishment. It's possible that the words they spoke to each other conveyed remorse—after all, they recalled Joseph's distress and pleading and their lack of response—but it was still too soon for Joseph to really know. Regardless, Joseph was undone and had to leave the room.

9. What do you think this moment was like for Joseph (verse 24)? Why do you think he wept?

Joseph enacted his plan by choosing Simeon, the second oldest brother, to be bound in front of the others and taken away. The text doesn't tell us why he chose Simeon. There are a couple of ideas, though.

First is that the oldest male in the family was traditionally the most valuable because he would lead the family and become the patriarch once the father died. Perhaps Joseph wanted to take the oldest in the family, but that would have been Reuben, the only brother who attempted to save Joseph from the pit. Since Reuben treated Joseph at least marginally better than the others, he possibly decided to honor that and instead chose Simeon, the next oldest.

Another reason that scholars speculate that Joseph chose Simeon was because perhaps Joseph believed the brothers valued Simeon least of all the other brothers, the same scenario Joseph had been in years ago. If the brothers hadn't changed and didn't really care about Simeon, they would likely repeat their actions and abandon their brother. If, however, they had changed, they would follow through on coming back to retrieve Simeon and return him to the family.

Joseph, in the midst of all his raw emotions, showed the brothers grace and mercy by giving them grain and provisions for their journey home. He also placed their silver, the money they should have used to purchase the grain they were taking home, back in their sacks. Either this could convey more grace on Joseph's part, or it could be a further test.

10. How did the brothers react when they found that the silver had been returned to one of the brothers (verse 28)? Why do you think finding the silver made them so afraid? Who did they worry was punishing them?

The brothers thought God was punishing them. It wasn't unreasonable for them to expect consequences for their actions. Sin always has consequences. However, God was not punishing the brothers. Punishment implies retribution, which goes against the character of God. God always has our best interest at heart and desires for us to become the people he created us to be. Thus, he will absolutely allow consequences for our sins to help us grow. And at times we are disciplined for what we have done.

Discipline is very different than punishment, though. Discipline is forward-looking—meaning it is intended to help us develop and become more Christlike in our character. Punishment just wants us to pay for what we have done, with no thought given to the development of who we are becoming. Discipline is what loving parents do with their children to help them make better choices moving forward. This also means that discipline doesn't always happen because we have done something wrong. Sometimes discipline is because God, just like a wise and loving parent, can see how we need to develop even before we wander off course.

Proverbs 3:11–12 sums up God's heart behind discipline this way: "My child, don't reject the LORD's discipline, and don't be upset when he corrects you. For the LORD corrects those he loves, just as a father corrects a child in whom he delights" (NLT).

"If you think of this world as a place intended simply for our happiness, you find it quite intolerable: think of it as a place of training and correction and it's not so bad."

—C. S. Lewis[2]

11. Reflect on a season or situation that was discipline for you. What happened? Read Hebrews 12:7–11. How do these verses reflect your experience with discipline? How did you grow in your relationship with the Lord as a result?

If you are still concerned that God may be a punishing God, look no further than Jesus to help alleviate those fears. Jesus died for us "while we were still sinners" (Romans 5:8). He didn't wait for us to clean up our act. The sin that you may still carry guilt over was paid for on the cross of Christ. While there are consequences for sin, you can be assured that your faith in Jesus means you will not be punished for that sin—or any other one. However, if you still carry a weight from something in your past, you may need to take some action to try to make things right. This is where the brothers never got back on track over those twenty-plus years Joseph was gone. They never told the truth, they never went looking for him, they never tried to make it right; instead, they tried to hide it and cover it up. The weight of their guilt was crushing.

12. Is there any weight of sin you carry from your past? If so, name that sin. Why do you think you have trouble letting go of this particular sin from your past? How do you think carrying the weight may be impacting your relationship with the Lord or others today?

13. Read Galatians 5:1 in the margin. How does this verse encourage you to let go of the burden you've been carrying because of your past sin?

"It is for freedom that Christ has set us free. Stand firm, then, and do not let yourselves be burdened again by a yoke of slavery."
—Galatians 5:1

14. As you consider the weight of sin you may be carrying from your past, take a few minutes to pray and ask God if there is something you should do to try to make it right on your end. Write down what comes to mind and make a plan to do this. If you've already done what you can or if there's no way to make it right, then turn it over to God and leave it in his hands. You do not need to feel guilt anymore. Go back to question 12 and write "I am free" over the sin you wrote about.

PRACTICE REMINDER

Before you start the lesson, take a few minutes
to write a prayer of lament for one of the
areas you identified in the practice section.

Day 4
Confronting Fear

Read Genesis 42:29–38.

The brothers, minus Simeon, returned home and reported what
had happened to their father, Jacob.

15. How did the brothers describe Joseph—still not knowing
    he was Joseph—and how he treated them (verses 29–34)?
    Does this description seem to support Joseph's original
    dreams in any way, and if so, how?

16. The brothers unpacked their bags from the journey and dis-
    covered that their silver had been returned to each of their
    sacks. What was their immediate response? Who, besides
    the brothers, was also frightened? Why do you think they
    responded this way?

17. Earlier the brothers stated to Joseph that "one is no more" (verse 13), which seemed to indicate that Joseph was dead. Considering this, why do you think Jacob used this phrase in verse 36 regarding Simeon? And why did he argue that he couldn't let Benjamin go (verses 36–38)?

18. What do you think Jacob's response says about him and his trust in God in this moment? Do you think Jacob's fear was unfounded or irrational? Why or why not? How might he have been letting fear overrun his life and decision-making? What impact do you think this had on him, Benjamin, and the other brothers?

19. Where do you tend to struggle with fear in your life? Why do you think this is?

20. Read the verses below and circle why we do not need to be afraid.

> Have I not commanded you? Be strong and courageous. Do not be afraid; do not be discouraged, for the LORD your God will be with you wherever you go. (Joshua 1:9)

> So do not fear, for I am with you; do not be dismayed, for I am your God. I will strengthen you and help you; I will uphold you with my righteous right hand. (Isaiah 41:10)

> Do not be anxious about anything, but in every situation, by prayer and petition, with thanksgiving, present your requests to God. And the peace of God, which transcends all understanding, will guard your hearts and your minds in Christ Jesus. (Philippians 4:6–7)

How do these verses encourage you to trust God even though you don't know what tomorrow holds? Specifically, what does Philippians 4:6–7 exhort us to do when we fear? Take a moment to pray and ask God to help you remember these truths whenever you are tempted by fear.

Present your requests to God.

P R A C T I C E   R E M I N D E R

Before you start the lesson, take a few minutes
to write a prayer of lament for one of the
areas you identified in the practice section.

Day 5
Trusting God's Promise

Read Genesis 43:1–14.

21. What happened that made Jacob reconsider sending his
    sons back to Egypt? Did he seem to forget about the condi-
    tions for their return? Why do you think this is?

22. Who guaranteed Benjamin's safety (verse 8; see also 42:37)?
    What do you think this says about if or how Judah and
    Reuben may have changed over the years?

If you have time, take a few minutes to go back and read Genesis 38. The chapter seems a little out of place, doesn't it? Chapter 37 draws us deep into the drama of Joseph's life and leaves us with the cliff-hanger that Joseph was sold as a slave. We expect the next chapter to continue telling us what happened to Joseph, but instead it jumps to Judah and tells the sordid story about his mistreatment of his daughter-in-law, Tamar. In an effort to guarantee a future for herself, she posed as a prostitute to trick Judah into providing for her as he should have done all along. At the end of this story, Judah declared, "She is more righteous than I" (38:26).

Judah's story in chapter 38 helps us understand why he responded as he did years later in chapter 43. Judah appeared to be a changed man. He was humbled by his wrongdoing. And here we see the fruit of his humility and growth. He guaranteed Benjamin's safety and declared he would assume the guilt for the rest of his life if Benjamin did not return safely home. We don't get the same backstory on Reuben, but we can assume he too has grown and changed for the good, since he also makes a promise and personal guarantee to bring Benjamin safely home.

Jacob decided returning to Egypt was the only way for the family to survive. In an effort to try to win the favor of "the man who is lord over the land" (42:30), he sent the best products from their land and twice as much silver to pay for the last batch of grain and hopefully to procure a second batch.

23. Considering Jacob and what he'd been through, how do you see him choosing to trust in the midst of his fears? Do you think he had any other options?

24. Jacob, like Joseph, also had a significant dream earlier in his life. Read Genesis 28:10–15. What did God promise Jacob in this dream? How do Jacob's actions and words in Genesis 43:11–14 indicate that he was choosing to remember these promises and trust God to fulfill them?

25. Match the following verses with some of the promises God makes to us as believers in Jesus today. Are there any additional promises you know of in Scripture that are encouraging to you? If so, write those below too.

John 10:10	Nothing can separate us from God's love.
Acts 1:11	Jesus is coming again.
Romans 8:38–39	When Jesus returns, we will live for eternity with no more death or pain.
1 Corinthians 3:16	The Holy Spirit lives in us.
Philippians 4:19	Jesus gives us abundant life now.
Revelation 21:4	God will meet all our needs.

26. What situation in your life do you need to choose to trust God more with, even though you are unsure of the outcome? Which of the promises from the previous question can you lean on and, like Jacob, choose to trust God with the outcome? Write a brief prayer to God, committing to trust him based on what he has promised you in Scripture.

Jacob's statement, "If I am bereaved, I am bereaved" (verse 14), reminds me of Queen Esther. Esther, who has an Old Testament book written about her, was an unlikely queen faced with the dangerous task of going before the king to beg for the lives of her people, the Jews. The king, who had not invited Esther into his court, could have reacted by having her killed. I know that sounds extreme, but truly it wasn't out of the realm of possibility based on his track record of erratic and emotionally driven behavior. There's a lot more to her story than I can summarize here, but trust me, it's a great story that is worthy of serious study. However, there's this defining moment in her life when she makes the bold, no-turning-back decision to go before the

If you are interested in diving into Esther's story, pick up a copy of *Crossroads: A Study of Esther and Jonah for Boldly Responding to Your Call.*

king. And in that moment, she declared, "If I perish, I perish" (Esther 4:16).

I love the declarations of both Jacob and Esther. With these words, they threw themselves, their lives, and their futures at the mercy of God. They affirmed with full force that they would do what they knew was right and trust God with the outcome. There was no promise that the outcome would be in their favor. There was a very real possibility that things would not work out as they wanted. And yet, they boldly trusted him anyway.

What a testimony to us. The truth is, life is often hard. If it's not right now, it will be someday sooner than we would like. We all know this is true. And yet, God has made some beautiful promises to us about our ultimate future. Promises we can rest in. Promises we can trust in. Promises that are true. I don't know what you are facing, but I'd guess there is a declaration you could make before boldly choosing to move forward and trust God with the outcome. Maybe it's that fear we turned over to him in question 19. If it's still creeping into your mind then take it before the Lord and declare boldly, "If it happens, it happens." And then remember all the promises that God makes, and choose to rest in the truth of these promises.

Friends, I know this to be true: God will never leave you or forsake you. He will be with you every step of the way—if you are bereaved, if you perish, if it happens. Whatever it is, he's got you. You can trust him.

PRACTICE REFLECTION

1. What did you choose to lament? Were there some prayers of lament (personal pain, national tragedy, or rampant injustice) that felt more natural to you than others? Why do you think that is?

2. How did this practice activity impact you this week?

3. How did it impact your relationship with God?

THE TEST

DAY 1

Practice—Laying Down Your Life

Alcoholism runs in my family. I have several family members who have battled the disease with varying levels of success. Some haven't done so well, some have. One family member in particular landed flat on her face and in treatment. She wondered if she had ruined her life. We wondered the same. I was scared when it all started to happen. What if she couldn't get on top of it? What if this round of treatment just led to another and another? We knew families that should have received punch cards to treatment centers for their repeat business. Their stories flooded my mind and made me fearful of the journey ahead. But off she went to battle her demons. And, as it turns out, there were many for her. She had to fight hard to reframe her thinking and then her life.

After treatment came the next hard step of learning to live a life of sobriety in a drinking-saturated world. She deconstructed piece after piece of her life. She stripped down her beliefs, wrestled with God, and eventually came out the other side. It was a long road. I've summarized it in a few sentences, but it was years and honestly, it's still in process.

As she started her journey, I wondered if she could do it. I wondered if she would wind up as another story of someone who limped along dragging the weight of their brokenness with them for the rest of their days. I wondered if it was possible for her to ever experience true freedom. Thankfully, she proved my wonderings wrong. She emerged from this experience transformed—a totally different person. She didn't even look the same. And it was all because of Jesus and her full and complete surrender to him and his will for her life. It was a hard-won freedom for her. If you ask her, she wouldn't take this terrible journey back because she now knows what it's like to live without lugging the baggage around. I wish her perspective was more common.

Have you ever witnessed a total transformation like this? Perhaps there's someone in your life and you've wondered if there is any hope for them. Maybe you even gave up on them, but somehow they found their way to a new life of freedom. They became a different person—they were truly transformed. Maybe that person is you. Praise God he doesn't ever give up on us. Praise God he does this kind of healing work in our lives. No one is beyond hope in his eyes.

Joseph's brother, Judah, is one such person who seemed beyond hope, but with God's help he found a new way to live and experienced full transformation. As we learned in the last lesson, the life-changing encounter with his daughter-in-law showed him the depth of his selfishness and sinfulness. This encounter landed him on his face and led him to become a different person. Joseph didn't know all that had happened to Judah, though. In fact, he didn't know if any of his brothers had changed or if they remained the same selfish men who threw him into the pit and sold him into slavery. Thus, the tests.

Joseph started this test as soon as he saw his brothers the first time (Genesis 42) and continued it when they arrived back in Egypt with baby brother Benjamin in tow. The bottom line of this test was to see if the brothers would abandon Benjamin as they had abandoned Joseph. I think he was hopeful that they had changed their ways, but I don't think he was ready for such a sacrificial gesture on the part of his brother Judah. Judah was ready to give his life for his brother. He was willing to sacrifice himself just to make sure his father didn't have to endure the loss of another beloved son.

We probably won't be called to make such a sacrifice on behalf of another, but we are called to daily lay down our lives for those around us. Jesus said it this way, "This is my commandment: Love each other in the same way I have loved you. There is no greater love than to lay down one's life for one's friends" (John 15:12–13 NLT). And it's not just our friends he tells us to do this for; he tells us to love our enemies too (Matthew 5:44). Oof. That's no easy task. How do we lay down our lives for others, especially those who are harder to love? First, we start by praying and asking God to help us be willing to take on the posture of a servant . . . just like Jesus did for us (Matthew 20:28). Next, we allow the Spirit to prompt us with practical ways we can lay down our lives.

This week for our practice, prayerfully consider the following questions, and then look for practical ways you could implement some of these ideas. This practice won't be easy. It's never easy to lay down our lives or our preferences for another person. But it is the way of Jesus.

- Where can I put someone's preferences ahead of my own?

- Is there someone I need to listen to without an agenda?

- Is there something I could go without so I could be generous to someone else?

- Is there any way I could serve someone's needs ahead of my own?

Before you start your lesson, pray, "Lord, help
me be aware of opportunities where I can
lay down my life for another today. Give me
courage to perform these acts out of love."

Day 2
Worst-Case Scenario

Read Genesis 43:15–23.

In the last lesson we finished the story with Joseph's father, Jacob,
staring his fear of losing his beloved youngest son, Benjamin, in
the face and declaring with boldness, "If I am bereaved, I am
bereaved" (verse 14). With that he sent his sons and the best gifts
he and the land had to offer to Egypt on a mission to hopefully
retrieve Simeon and procure food for their survival.

1. When Joseph saw his brothers, what did he do (verse
   16)? Why do you think he did this? How did the brothers
   respond?

> *Joseph told the steward to bring them into the house, slaughter an animal for the men to dine w/ him. They were afraid he wd. be upset ab. the money*

Genesis 41:57 told us, "All the world came to Egypt to buy grain
from Joseph, because the famine was severe everywhere." We can
presume from this statement that Joseph had to meet with many
travelers to decide if and how much grain he would sell them.
The text doesn't tell us, but I would imagine the brothers stood
in some sort of line to wait their turn to talk to Joseph. And

then Joseph looked up and saw them, leaned over to his steward, and told him to take the men to his house for a noon meal. This frightened the brothers. Why were they singled out? Why did he treat them differently than all the others who had come to buy food? The brothers don't know the answers to these questions, but they immediately assumed the worst.

2. What did the brothers assume was going to happen (Genesis 43:18)? Why do you think they assumed this (consider also Genesis 42:21–22, 28)?

3. Fear has a way of making us vividly imagine worst-case scenarios, then experience overwhelming emotions, as if those scenarios are actually happening to us. This is exactly what the brothers did. What is an area of your life where you experience fear? How have you let your imagination run away with this fear, like the brothers did? How has this kind of thinking impacted you? How has it impacted your relationship with the Lord?

"Worrying is carrying tomorrow's load with today's strength— carrying two days at once. It is moving into tomorrow ahead of time. Worrying doesn't empty tomorrow of its sorrow, it empties today of its strength."

—Corrie ten Boom[1]

4. Have you found any ways to help you overcome worst-case scenario and fear-based thinking? What have you tried that has worked?

If you are struggling to get this type of thinking under control, write down some of the ideas your group shares and put them into practice.

5. Read Exodus 16:4 and Matthew 6:9–11. (In the Exodus passage, the Israelites had fled slavery in Egypt and were on their way to the promised land.) What do these verses teach us about trusting God? How do these verses help you surrender your fears for tomorrow to his care?

6. What did the brothers do to confront their fear (Genesis 43:19–22)? What did they learn (verse 23)? How do you think this made them feel?

☀

A close reading of Genesis 42:28 and verse 35 tells us that one brother found the silver on the way home, and then they discovered their silver had been returned to all of them when they were unpacking their bags at home with their father. Yet here in Genesis 43:21, the brothers make it sound like they found their silver on the way home instead of at two different times. Why the discrepancy? It's hard to say, but it seems like the brothers are compressing the story for the steward. We do this today when we combine multiple conversations or events into one detail. Usually, we do this not with the intent to lie or trick our listeners but to simply move the story forward with expediency. I think this is what the brothers were doing here.

•••••••

After this quick conversation and reassurance, the steward brought Simeon out and reunited him with his brothers. We don't know how long Simeon was in prison, but we can assume it was at least weeks if not months. We gather this from the fact that during the first trip to Egypt the brothers were given enough grain to fill large sacks that their donkeys carried home for them (42:25–26). It wasn't until after they had exhausted all their grain that Jacob even considered sending them back to Egypt to try to get more food (43:1–2). All the while, Simeon sat and waited. He was well aware of how long the trip would take. He marked the days waiting. As they began to stretch beyond a reasonable length of time for the round trip, surely he started to wonder if they would ever return, well aware of the fact that they never went after Joseph. I'm guessing Joseph began to wonder the same thing for Simeon. The more days that went by, the more it probably fed Joseph's false narrative that nothing had changed for his brothers, who would be willing to leave someone behind if it was better for the rest of them.

P R A C T I C E   R E M I N D E R

Before you start your lesson, pray, "Lord, help me be aware of opportunities where I can lay down my life for another today. Give me courage to perform these acts out of love."

Day 3
Preferential Treatment

Read Genesis 43:24–34.

7. Compare Genesis 37:5–7 with 43:26. What do you notice? Do you think Joseph realized this?

Joseph was seventeen when he was taken from his family, which means he was seventeen when he last saw his baby brother. We don't know how old Benjamin was, but he was probably a young child. Twenty years would have changed Benjamin a lot.

8. What did Joseph do after he was given confirmation that the new person with them was Benjamin (verses 30–31)? Imagine this scene for a moment. What do you think this was like for the brothers? What do you think it was like for Joseph?

9. There are multiple things that happen in Genesis 43 that should have seemed odd to the brothers. Fill in the chart below, identifying these things and how they reacted to them. I've done the first one for you.

Verse	What happened	Reaction by brothers (if stated)
16	Joseph told steward to take them to his house for a meal	Overblown fear as to why Joseph would do this (verse 18)
23		
30		
33		
34		

When Joseph gave Benjamin a portion that was five times as large as everyone else's, he was clearly favoring Benjamin by giving him preferential treatment.

10. Why do you think Joseph gave Benjamin more food than
    everyone else? How did this act of favoring Benjamin mimic
    the broken family dynamic Joseph experienced as a child?
    How could this have been another part of the test Joseph
    had devised to learn about his brothers?

11. How do you tend to react when someone is given prefer-
    ential treatment in your presence? How do you tend to re-
    act when you are the one given the preferential treatment?
    Read Romans 12:10 below. Underline the two actions we
    are encouraged to do for others. What are some practical
    ways you can do these things?

"Be devoted to one another in love. Honor one another
above yourselves."

—Romans 12:10

12. We know the real story of why Joseph did all these things, but the brothers were still clueless and had no idea who Joseph really was. Why do you think they were able to finally relax at the meal with Joseph so they could feast and drink freely with him (verse 34)?

PRACTICE REMINDER

Before you start your lesson, pray, "Lord, help
me be aware of opportunities where I can
lay down my life for another today. Give me
courage to perform these acts out of love."

Day 4
The Final Test

Read Genesis 44:1–31.

13. Briefly summarize what the final test was that Joseph con-
    ducted. Why do you think he had the cup placed in Benja-
    min's sack?

14. What did the brothers say they would do if they were found
    with the silver cup (verse 9)? Why do you think they made
    such an extreme offer for punishment? What did the stew-
    ard then say he would do (verse 10)? Why do you think he
    made the punishment different than what they offered?

When the cup was found in Benjamin's sack, the brothers tore their clothes, which is an ancient sign of extreme distress or grief. Then they all returned to Egypt to face Joseph together. When they saw Joseph, Judah became the spokesperson for the group and offered that they would all become his slaves. Joseph, of course, rejected this offer and made the final offer that only Benjamin needed to stay and the rest of them could return to their father in Canaan.

15. How did the offer Joseph made to the brothers mimic what they did to Joseph when he was seventeen? If they left Benjamin behind, what would that show Joseph? If they wouldn't leave him behind, what would that show Joseph?

At this, Judah made a bold appeal to Joseph by recounting their painful family story. He told Joseph that losing Benjamin would cause so much pain and suffering that it would almost certainly kill their elderly father.

16. Is there anything that Judah left out of the story he told Joseph in verses 18–29? Why do you think he left this out? Do you think Benjamin knew the whole story?

While Judah left out some very important details in his account of what happened to the "dead" brother (verse 20), it does seem that Judah and the other brothers had changed.

17. Is there a relationship in your life that had previously been damaged but the person changed, and you were able to rebuild some form of relationship with them? If so, what happened? How did your relationship with God play a role in your ability to move forward in some way with this person? If trust was fully restored, how did that happen? If you have had a relationship broken because of something someone did to you, what would it take to have trust restored in that person?

Please note: sometimes restoration means forgiveness but not reconciliation, especially in abusive situations. God can do miraculous work in the lives of broken people—he has certainly done it in mine, and I'm guessing he has done it in yours too. And while he can even redeem abusive situations to make them safe and loving again, we are not often called to move back into those relationships.

PRACTICE REMINDER

Before you start your lesson, pray, "Lord, help
me be aware of opportunities where I can
lay down my life for another today. Give me
courage to perform these acts out of love."

Day 5
The Great Exchange

Read Genesis 44:32–34.

18. What did Judah ask Joseph to do? What would this mean
    for Judah and the rest of his life? Why do you think he
    made such an extreme offer? What do you think Joseph
    was thinking and feeling when Judah made his offer?

It's interesting to note that neither Benjamin nor the brothers ever
claimed innocence. In fact, we don't even know if Judah thought
Benjamin was innocent or guilty. I'm guessing they discussed it
on the way back to the city, but even if Judah believed Benjamin
was innocent it didn't really matter. The evidence had been found
and they knew they were powerless foreigners who had to answer
to a powerful official.

What Judah did is stunning. He offered his life for another.
He offered to bear the penalty for something he definitely did
not do so the "guilty" one could go free. In this instance, Judah

was acting like a Christ figure by modeling what Jesus did for us. Let's walk through Jesus's sacrifice and why it was necessary.

19. According to Romans 3:9–18 and 23, who is guilty and why? Do you agree with this? Why or why not?

This is hard news. Every single one of us is tainted with the disease of sin. Just by being human, we inherit this condition. Our experience tells us this is true. Even people who are "good" are not perfect. And the standard is perfection. It's a standard we cannot meet.

20. According to Romans 6:23, what is just payment for our sin? What is the gift of God? Considering this, what do you think "death" means in this verse?

21. Read 2 Corinthians 5:21 and 1 Peter 2:24. What exactly did Jesus do for us? And what does he give us in exchange? Finally, according to Romans 10:9–10 and Ephesians 2:8–9 (see next page), what must we do to be saved?

"For it is by grace you have been saved, through faith—and this is not from yourselves, it is the gift of God—not by works, so that no one can boast."

—Ephesians 2:8–9

Second Corinthians 5:21 is sometimes referred to as "the great exchange" because it unpacks the rich truth that Christ not only takes our sin but also gives us his righteousness. That means we, as followers of Jesus, take on the righteousness of Christ. That's hard to wrap our minds around. He doesn't just pay for our sin to bring us back to a zero balance so we can work hard from there. No, he actually gives us his righteousness and empowers us to live differently moving forward.

22. Take a moment to reflect upon the great exchange Jesus made for you. How do you feel knowing that someone literally laid down their life for you? What does it mean for you to now have the righteousness of Christ? How does this impact how you live? Write out a prayer of thanksgiving to God for what he has done for you.

If you have not yet become a follower of Jesus by accepting this truth about him, prayerfully consider doing so now. It will be the best decision you'll ever make. If you do make this declaration in faith, make sure you tell your small group leader, a Christian friend, or a pastor so they can help you learn what it means to grow as a follower of Jesus.

23. Think about Judah again. Is there anything that would ever lead you to make an offer to lay down your life for another person like he did? Why or why not?

Judah made an extraordinary offer to Joseph—his life for Benjamin's freedom. I can't imagine this is how Joseph thought his test would play out. He probably thought they would ask for Benjamin's release and then abandon Benjamin when Joseph said no. Or maybe, if they had really changed, they'd throw themselves at his feet and beg for mercy as they declared their innocence— perhaps even offering some form of reparation. But a life for a life? This had to be stunning to Joseph. It was unexpected. It was extravagant. It revealed a true change of heart.

In the next lesson, we will see how Joseph responded. It's the moment we've all been waiting for!

PRACTICE REFLECTION

1. In what ways did you lay down your life by sacrificially serving another this week? What happened?

2. Were there opportunities to lay down your life through sacrificial service and you resisted? What happened?

3. What did this practice teach you about yourself? What did this practice teach you about God?

IN GOD'S TIME

DAY 1
Practice—Silence

I've never been good at waiting. And yet, I feel like my days are always marked by waiting. Waiting until I turned sixteen so I could drive, counting down the days to graduation, waiting in anticipation for a big day to finally arrive, watching the clock slowly—ever so slowly—tick by waiting for the call . . . wait, wait, wait. Why does time seem to slow in the waiting? Please tell me the same is true for you.

Part of the reason I'm not good at waiting is I like to make things happen. Be in control. Waiting is a total loss of control. It's a place where I'm at the mercy of someone or something else. Today I'm in a place of waiting. I'm waiting for an important email to be returned. I'm waiting for a package to arrive. I'm waiting for the Lord's leading on a new direction I feel like he's nudging me toward. I'm waiting on a season of disruption to return to normalcy, whatever that means. I'm waiting. Always waiting.

Actually, we should be waiting. Waiting is biblical. Now, before you throw your book across the room in protest, hear me out. Scripture tells us we should be waiting *on the Lord*. Psalm 27:14 says it this way, "Wait for the LORD; be strong and take heart and wait for the LORD." I'm not sure God could be any more clear. We are to be waiting people. Waiting on God to lead us (Proverbs 3:6), waiting on God to return for us (Matthew 24:36–42), waiting on God to set all things right (Revelation 21:4–5). And so, we wait. But don't get me wrong; we don't just sit around and watch the clock. No, we've got good work to do in the meantime (Ephesians 2:10).

By now you know that Joseph didn't get a pass on waiting. It is, in fact, one of the major themes of Joseph's life. He waited in a foreign country, waited as a slave, waited in prison, waited in need. And then one day he found himself in abundance and with a position of power and honor—but he was still waiting. He waited twenty-two years in total for his God-given dream to come to fruition. And while he waited, he trusted. There was really no other good option. He could trust in God and his good plans—even in the midst of incredibly confusing uncertainty—or he could abandon all hope and succumb to his circumstances. I wonder if he would have even survived if he had chosen that. We don't have to wonder because Joseph was steadfast and resilient. He chose to trust God in the waiting. Day after day after day. Oh, to be a little more like Joseph (sans the prison and suffering, please).

To help us grow in our ability to wait, we need to exercise our waiting muscles. That means we need to impose it on ourselves. A great way to do this is through the practice of silence and still-ness. It's counterintuitive to my natural way of doing, fixing, and controlling, but when I sit in stillness and silence with the Lord it reminds my soul that he is God and I am not. He doesn't need my striving; rather, he requests my waiting and my willingness to fol-low his lead when he reveals it. Silence and stillness are incredibly simple, yet incredibly hard to practice. In fact, if you're anything like me, this might be one of the hardest practices I invite you to do. It's hard to be still in a task-driven world. It's hard to do something that feels like nothing. It's hard to settle our minds and let them rest in the Lord's presence.

This practice of being silent is not with the goal of empty-ing our minds. That's more akin to an Eastern, non-Christian meditation practice and not at all what we are doing. Instead, our goal is to sit still and quiet in the presence of God. This practice is also different than our prayer time because we aren't talking to God. We are in more of a listening posture. God may nudge you in this time with a thought, a conviction, or a direction he wants you to take, but he may also feel very quiet. Either is OK.

Here are a few tips to help you get started with the practice of being still. First, find a quiet place and sit in an attentive posture so you don't fall asleep . . . not that I've ever done that. Next, choose a name of God, such as Father, Savior, or Redeemer, or a short verse to bring to mind for when your mind wanders. These are some of my favorite verses:

- 1 Samuel 3:10—"Speak, for your servant is listening."
- Psalm 23:1—"The LORD is my shepherd, I lack nothing."
- Psalm 46:10—"Be still, and know that I am God."

I like to recite the verse a few times at the beginning of my time and then when my mind wanders, I'll go back to a word or two from the verse to help me settle in again. Finally, set a timer. I recommend you start with five minutes. The timer will help you relax and avoid peeking at the clock to see how long you've been sitting in silence.

I want to warn you about something that will most likely happen as you do this practice: random thoughts will jump into your mind, and I mean random. A box you think could be in the attic—you should probably see if it's still there. That friend from twenty years ago—you need to find them on social media right away. A random item from the grocery store—you should go out and get it now, so you don't forget. The best thing to do when these crazy ideas jump into your mind is either let them go or quickly jot them down. When I practice silence, I turn to the back page of my journal and write all the random things there. Interestingly, almost none of them really matter. They are all just distractions to keep me from being present with God.

And that is the goal. We aren't trying to get anything from God, just be present with God. The whole point is to remind our

souls that God is God and we are not. As you do this practice, I
hope you find that waiting on God isn't all that bad and, in fact,
it's better than any alternative we have. Joseph is a great example
to us in this.

Make some decisions about your time of being still, and make
notes below.

- What verse or name of God will you use to help you settle
  into your time of stillness and silence? Write it below.

"Speak, for your servant is listening."

- What physical place could you do this practice and what
  time of day would be best? Consider setting a reminder
  alarm on your phone to help you remember to do this practice daily this week.

mornings or night

- If you are able, set a timer right now and take five minutes
  to be still and silent with the Lord. Write what your experience was like.

Take five minutes to be silent and
still with the Lord today.

Day 2
The Revelation

Read Genesis 45:1–24.

Joseph was undone. He completed his tests, and through them
discovered that his brothers had in fact changed. Judah was willing to lay down his life for his brother. And with this revelation,
Joseph could no longer hold back. He cried out to his attendants,
"Leave!" Everyone left except the brothers and Joseph.

The brothers had no idea what was happening. The man in
front of them started weeping—loudly and uncontrollably. On
the surface it had to seem laughably unprofessional. But there
was no laughter, and they were terrified. What was happening?
What was this man going to do?

Joseph collected himself enough to cobble together the words
he had longed to say for years, "I am Joseph!"

They stared back in stunned silence. *Wait, what? What did he
just say? It's not possible. There's just no way. It's been twenty-
two years.* They thought he was dead.

1. After Joseph revealed his identity, how did he try to reassure his brothers (verses 5–8)? Why do you think he tried
   to reassure them?

*- You do this for someone you care
about. Healthy or not, it seems
like he does this out of concern
+ care for his brothers.*

2. Who did Joseph say sent him to Egypt (verse 8)? Does this excuse the sinful action of the brothers selling Joseph as a slave? Why or why not? Do you think God could have gotten Joseph to Egypt another way? Imagine what could have been a different scenario.

> God sent me to Egypt — to preserve life.
> ... "to preserve a remnant on earth.
>
> No it does not excuse the sin + yes
> God could have gotten him there another
> way.

3. Joseph then instructed the brothers to hurry home and get Jacob and the rest of the family. What did Joseph say he would do for them when they returned (verses 9–11)? Why did he say this was necessary (verses 7 and 11)?

> You shall dwell in the land of
> Goshen + be near me. There I
> will provide for you (and your family)

4. God knew when and where the famine would happen. He also knew his people would be threatened by this severe crisis. Thus, he started twenty-two years before this moment to ensure all the right pieces were in all the right places. What was God's ultimate goal (verse 7)? Why do you think he allowed these events to unfold in the first place? How do you think this long journey ultimately impacted Joseph and the brothers' relationships with one another and with God?

> To preserve a __remnant__ on earth
>   (yether "what is leftover"

✳

"God doesn't manufacture pain, but he certainly puts it to use."
—Max Lucado[1]

5. What might have been lost if God fixed everything twenty-two years earlier and prevented the famine altogether? Consider some of the longer and harder circumstances you have endured. How have these journeys changed you? What might have been the result for you if you never had to go through them?

Pain grows us up + often forces our gaze to God.

Keep in mind that while God allows difficult circumstances, like he did with Joseph, he never desires for us to sin or be caught in another's sin. What the brothers did was wrong and the consequences for them and Joseph were lasting. Sin is never God's will for our lives. However, God can and will use these hard circumstances to teach us, discipline us, and help us move toward becoming more like him.

6. Read Proverbs 3:5–6 and Isaiah 40:31 (in the margin). What do these verses teach us about trusting God in uncertain times? What is one way, big or small, that you need to trust God today? How does remembering what he did for you in the past, as well as reflecting on these verses, help you trust him now?

"But those who trust in the LORD will find new strength. They will soar high on wings like eagles. They will run and not grow weary. They will walk and not faint."
—Isaiah 40:31 (NLT)

> *If we trust Him, He shows up on our behalf.*

Pharaoh was happy to hear that Joseph's family was alive and well. He encouraged the brothers to get the rest of the family to Egypt so they could enjoy the "fat of the land" and "the best of all Egypt" (Genesis 45:18, 20). Joseph gathered gifts, provisions, and carts to help with transportation back to Egypt and then sent them off with this final exhortation, "Don't quarrel on the way" (verse 24).

What might they quarrel about? Well, from what we've seen in how they have responded to one another in previous chapters, what wouldn't they quarrel about? However, there's also some debate if "quarrel" is really the best translation based on the context of the original Hebrew. It's also possible to translate the word as "stir up." And the New English Translation Bible suggests that based on other uses of the word, for example in Exodus 15:14, it might be better to translate Joseph's phrase as "don't be afraid."[2] If this is the case, he might be telling them not to stir up or get agitated with fear about coming back to Egypt because he wouldn't seek retribution for their actions, therefore they didn't need to fear him.

Either way seems to work based on what we've seen of the brothers. They had indeed changed, but they still struggled with what they had done, and this made their interactions ripe for both quarreling and fear.

Take five minutes to be silent and
still with the Lord today.

Day 3
Promises

Read Genesis 45:25–46:7.

7. According to Genesis 45:25–28, what was Jacob's initial
   reaction to the revelation that Joseph was alive? What convinced him? Why do you think this was convincing?

> Joseph's words + wagons are
> what convinced him.
>
> • Initially his heart became
>   numb + he did not believe
>   him.

Jacob, also called Israel, gathered the family and their possessions and set off toward Egypt. On the way, he made a stop in
Beersheba to offer sacrifices to the Lord. There he had a powerful
encounter with God that reminded him of the promises God had
made in the past.

8. Look up the following verses and fill in the chart on the
   next page regarding the covenant promise God made in the
   past to his people starting with Abraham. (Note: this is
   called the Abrahamic covenant.)

Verse	Who God is speaking to	What God promised	Who would be blessed through their offspring
Genesis 12:1-3	Abraham (Jacob's grandfather, called Abram in this passage) + those who dishonor ~~title~~ you I will curse.	"I will make you a great nation + I will bless you + make your name great, so you will be a blessing. I will bless those who bless you	all the families of the earth shall be blessed!"
Genesis 26:2-4	Isaac (Jacob's father)	I will be with you + bless you, + give your offspring these lands + establish the Oath I swore to Abraham.	"in your offspring all the nations of the earth shall be blessed."
Genesis 28:13-14	Jacob (also called Israel)	I will give you the land on which you lie. Your offspring shall be like the dust of the earth.	"all the families of the earth shall be blessed."

Why do you think God repeated the promise to Isaac and Jacob?

9. How would God ultimately bless everyone through the off-spring of Abraham (Matthew 1:1)? How does this mean you are included in the Abrahamic covenant and have benefited from the journey of Jacob and Joseph? How does knowing the grand scope of this story give you a different perspective on the devastation both Jacob and Joseph went through?

10. What does God tell Jacob in Genesis 46:3–4? What is similar between this promise and the one God previously made to him back in Genesis 28:13–14? What is different? Why do you think Jacob needed to hear these words from God?

*land is missing

I am God, the God of your father. DO not be afraid to go down to Egypt, for there I will make you a great nation.

Jacob, when he received the first promise from God in Genesis 28, was a much younger man. He had not married or had any children yet. A lot had transpired in Jacob's life between that first encounter with God and the one we read about in Genesis 46. We don't know for sure, but it's plausible that Jacob struggled to trust God after the loss of his beloved son Joseph and wife Rachel, especially when you consider how he clung to Benjamin and placed an inordinate amount of value on him and his life (Genesis 42:38). Jacob was even willing to let the entire extended family starve for fear of losing Benjamin. Of course, this plan would also backfire if Benjamin starved to death with the rest of the family. I wonder if in the midst of these impossible decisions Jacob recalled the promise and realized God couldn't make his offspring like the "dust of the earth" (28:14) if they couldn't even survive until the next harvest. Perhaps it was this realization that emboldened him to take the risk and trust God enough to release his beloved Benjamin.

Jacob may have been struggling to trust God, but God remained trustworthy. His promise remained steadfast and true because it wasn't dependent upon Jacob's, or anyone's, faith or faithfulness—it was solely dependent upon God. Jacob didn't know what God had been doing behind the scenes. He may have believed they were out of options, but God was orchestrating the perfect plan to save them and, ultimately, you and me.

✗ Just like Jacob, when we can't see our way out of a mess or hard time, we need to remember that God has not stopped working. And we can rest in his provision and his promises.

Here are a few of his promises to remember:

Your eternity in heaven is secure (John 3:16).
Nothing you do will ever separate you from God or his love for you (Romans 8:38–39).
✗ You are forgiven because of his grace, not your good works (Ephesians 2:8–9).
God will meet all your needs (Philippians 4:19).
Even when we are faithless, God remains faithful (2 Timothy 2:13).

He will never leave you or forsake you (Hebrews 13:5).
He forgives all your sins (1 John 1:9).

11. What promise from God do you need to remember today
    and why? (Feel free to choose from the list above or from
    another verse you may know.) Look up the verse and write
    it out, inserting your name where you can. (For example, I
    could write: "Jodie, I will never leave you or forsake you.")
    Take a few minutes to reflect on this promise and then write
    a short prayer to God praising him for this truth and what
    it means to you today.

The LORD will meet all
your needs.

PRACTICE REMINDER

Take five minutes to be silent and
still with the Lord today.

Day 4
Reunion and Resettling

Read Genesis 46:26–47:10.

After Jacob had his encounter with God, he set off to Egypt with
the entire family. The text tells us that sixty-six direct descendants
made the journey. It doesn't count the sons' wives, not because
they didn't matter, but because the genealogy went through the
male line.

The family arrived in Goshen and sent Judah ahead to get
directions. As soon as Joseph heard they were close, he rode out
to meet them.

12. What did Joseph do when he saw Jacob (Genesis 46:29–
    30)? What did Jacob say to Joseph? What do you think
    this reunion was like? What do you think the brothers ex-
    perienced as they looked upon Joseph and Jacob's tearful
    reunion?

fell on his neck + wept.

Pain, shame, sorrow

13. What did Joseph instruct the brothers to do (verses 31–34)? What did Egyptians think of shepherds? What do you think this means about the land of Goshen?

14. Knowing that Egyptians held a biased and unfavorable view of shepherds, what are some of the things the brothers might have worried about as they went to meet Pharaoh, who was probably the most powerful man alive at the time? How do you think their actions showed that they trusted God? How did their actions show that they trusted Joseph? What was the end result (47:5–6)?

They were able to settle in the land of Goshen.

With the declaration that Egyptians found shepherds detestable, we find proof that the fallen human heart has been imaginative from the beginning of time in how it creates and shows prejudice, which can quickly lead toward subjugation. We see it happen here; in three short chapters Genesis ends and Exodus begins with these shepherds as slaves.

....

15. What are some biases and prejudices people hold against others today? Where do you think these biases stem from? How do they impact the people who are held in bias?

16. Prayerfully ask the Lord to help you see what biases you hold in your heart. What comes to mind? Why do you think you have this bias toward this person or group of people? What is one practical thing you can do to help you overcome this bias and see others more as God sees them?

Take five minutes to be silent and
still with the Lord today.

Day 5
What Really Matters

Read Genesis 47:11–27.

17. According to verses 11–12, what did Joseph do next? How
    does this contrast to verse 13?

18. Fill in the blanks for how the Egyptians had to procure
    food.

    First, the Egyptians gave their _____ for the grain
    (verse 14).
    Next, the Egyptians gave their _____ for the grain
    (verses 16–17).
    Next, the Egyptians gave their _____ (verse 20)
    and _____ (verse 21) for the grain.
    The Egyptians gave _____ of their crop to Pharaoh
    (verse 24).

What could they do with the rest of the crop?

How did the Egyptians respond to Joseph (verse 25)? Why do you think this was their response when they had lost so much?

The Egyptians had to keep choosing between a rock and a hard place. Give all their money or starve. Give all their livestock or starve. Give all their land or starve. Give themselves in servitude or starve. There were no easy answers and no good alternatives. They were destitute and on the brink of death—all they had to give they gave. The only one who really fared well in this whole situation was Pharaoh. He came out owning all the money, livestock, land, and people. The wealth and power of an already wealthy and powerful man just increased all the more. And all because of the wisdom and leadership of Joseph.

But, surprisingly, the people were grateful. They were happy to come out with their lives because the alternative was worse. This crisis helped them shift their perspective to what was really important. Crisis has a way of doing this. It strips away all the things we thought were important and puts into focus what really matters.

19. Think of a specific crisis or hard time you've gone through. How did it help you focus on what was really important? What did it put in perspective for you? What is one thing you can do today to show someone who is important to you

that they matter more than other less important things that can tend to distract you? Make a plan to do this thing in the next twenty-four hours.

20. Thinking about what has happened so far in Joseph's story, how did God use the twenty-two years that Joseph was separated from his family to prepare him for this moment? What does this teach you about God's timing?

21. What are you waiting for in your life—perhaps marriage, children, a career, retirement, a new opportunity, a re-stored relationship, healing, or something else? How does reflecting on the length of time it took for Joseph's journey help you trust God with the timing of what you are waiting for? How does reflecting on Joseph's journey help you trust God even if what you are waiting for never happens?

22. According to verse 27, while the Egyptians were barely surviving the famine, what was happening to the Israelites? What seems odd about this? Look back at question 8 (on page 152) and recall the Abrahamic covenant that God made to Abraham and then repeated to Isaac and Jacob. What parts of God's promise does verse 27 reflect?

I don't want you to miss this, so I'm also going to add some information to help you answer the question I just asked. The Abrahamic promise was for the future, but it was also for the people in that moment. John Walton, author and theologian, states, "The time in Egypt is not an interruption of the covenant but an incubation of the covenant people."[3] During this incubation period, God not only protected his people from demise but also graced them with the ability to flourish. While the Egyptians had to sell their property so they could live, the people of Israel, who were foreigners and guests in the land, were provided with both property and food. It's completely counterintuitive. It shouldn't have happened this way and yet it did. This is our God.

You may be facing your own challenging season, and much like the Israelites you feel uprooted and like you've been placed in a foreign land. Perhaps this season can become a season of flourishing for you too. Ask God to show you how you can seek him for thriving even in the midst of what you are facing.

PRACTICE REFLECTION

1. What was sitting in silence daily with the Lord like for you?
   What did you notice while you were doing this practice?

2. Did you learn anything new about God or waiting on God
   as a result of this practice?

FINAL AND FULL FORGIVENESS

DAY 1
Practice—Extending Forgiveness

If only Dad hadn't favored me in such a showy way.

If only I had kept those dreams to myself.

If only that caravan of Ishmaelites hadn't come at that exact moment.

If only Reuben had been there and convinced the rest of my brothers not to sell me.

If only . . .

Then maybe my brothers wouldn't have hated me.

Then maybe they wouldn't have sold me as a slave.

Then maybe I wouldn't have missed out on the life I should have had with my family.

Then maybe.

It's a dangerous road to go down. *If only, then maybe.* But that's what our brain does, doesn't it? It likes to revisit the past and imagine what could have been *if only.* And then romanticize the future with thoughts of *then maybe.*

If only . . . then maybe. What's your "if only, then maybe"?

And more pertinent to where we are in Joseph's story, who created an "if only, then maybe" scenario for you?

For Joseph it was his brothers. They tried to destroy his life. They ripped his promising future right out of his hands. He was powerless and they were powerful. He was beaten, cast aside, sold as property . . . you know the story. How could he possibly forgive them for such an overt atrocity?

We may not have faced such a terrible or wounding betrayal as Joseph, but we too have people we need to fully and finally forgive. How do we do this? The first step is understanding what forgiveness is and isn't. Let's start with what forgiveness isn't. It isn't turning a blind eye to what has been done. It isn't pretending that you weren't hurt. And it definitely isn't going back into an abusive situation. So then, what is forgiveness? According to Berkeley University, forgiveness is "a conscious, deliberate decision to release feelings of resentment or vengeance toward a person or group who has harmed you," even when they don't really deserve it.[1] Releasing someone is no easy task. We have to decide to forgive—even when it isn't deserved. Even when we can't continue in the relationship.

Author and researcher Brené Brown also states that forgiveness begins with death. Meaning we need to grieve our "if only, then maybe" before we can move forward. Once we have done that, we can move through a process of forgiveness she outlines that includes "telling the story, naming the hurt, granting forgiveness, and renewing or releasing the relationship."[2] It is hard and difficult work to do, but it is tied to our emotional, mental, and physical well-being, which means it is work worth doing. And as believers, it is work we are called to do. We are to extend forgiveness because we have been forgiven. Colossians 3:13 says it this way, "Bear with each other and forgive one another. . . . Forgive as the Lord forgave you." God extends grace and forgiveness to us that we did nothing to earn. And he asks us to show a similar grace and forgiveness to others.

This extravagant and undeserved forgiveness process is exactly what we see Joseph model: "'You intended to harm me, but God intended it for good to accomplish what is now being done, the saving of many lives. So then, don't be afraid. I will provide for you and your children.' And he reassured them and spoke kindly to them" (Genesis 50:20–21).

Packed into these few words, we see him let go of the past, tell his story, and name the truth of the hurt, but then also grant forgiveness and, because his brothers showed they had changed, renew his relationship with his brothers. It's a powerful example for us to follow.

But don't for a minute think it was easy. Releasing feelings of resentment or vengeance toward another is difficult, near miraculous. It's work we need God's help with. Joseph's declaration, "You intended to harm me, but God intended it for good" (verse 20), shows that God stepped in and helped him reframe what had happened. We'll get into this more as we study the passage for the week, but quickly you need to note that he did not say what happened was good—but that God used it for good. Even the worst things that have happened in our lives, God can, and will, use for our good. It doesn't mean those things are good. It just means that our God is able to take brokenness and make it into something beautiful.

This week for our practice, I want to invite you to follow Joseph's lead and forgive . . . even if it isn't deserved. To start, begin with praying and asking God who he wants you to forgive. Once you know who you need to forgive, ask the Lord to help you grieve the "if only, then maybe" of the situation. Then take some time to prayerfully write the story of what happened and name the hurt. If you feel you need to bring someone into this process with you, ask the Lord who that should be and heed any nudges he gives you. It's important to be careful who you tell your story to so that it doesn't become gossip or cause more hurt. A trusted Christian friend who does not know the offending person is probably best. Then make the intentional decision to release them by extending full forgiveness to them. If you are inviting a friend on this journey with you, ask your friend to pray with you and for you as you do this. At this point, you will then need to decide if you release or renew the relationship with the person who hurt you.

The process may be simple, but the implementation is difficult. To do this practice you will need to spend some intentional time in prayer and reflection. Take your time moving through these steps over the next few days. I will give you reminders each day to help you. And when you complete this process and have made the decision to release someone in full forgiveness, don't be surprised when the memory of the offense creeps back into your mind. When it does, remind yourself you have released that person in full forgiveness and then ask the Lord to help you see how he has or can use the offense for your good as he promises to do.

"When it comes to forgiveness, all of us are beginners. No one owns a secret formula. As long as you are trying to forgive, you are forgiving. It's when you no longer try that bitterness sets in."

—Max Lucado[3]

If Joseph could forgive his brothers for what they had done, I believe you can extend forgiveness too. Take some time right now to start the process.

Pray and ask the Lord to bring to mind names and situations you need to forgive. Write down anything that comes to mind. (Feel free to write in code.) With the Lord's help, choose one person you will seek to forgive this week.

PRACTICE REMINDER

Before you start your lesson, take a few
minutes to begin writing your story and naming
the hurt that you are seeking to forgive.

Day 2
Fear of Retribution

Before we dive into today's lesson, I want to take a minute to bridge
the gap for why we are skipping over Genesis 47:28–50:14. This
part of the story, while still including Joseph, shifts the focus onto
his father, Jacob, and his final days. Most of the passage is about
Jacob's patriarchal blessing bestowed upon Joseph's sons, Manasseh
and Ephraim, in chapter 48, and then upon his twelve sons in chapter 49. While these chapters are interesting, they can also be confusing. Since they don't further the story of Joseph significantly, we
aren't going to spend time digging into them in any depth.

At the end of Genesis 49 Jacob dies. Genesis 50 begins with the
family mourning in Egypt and then caravanning to Canaan to bury
Jacob. Once they return to Egypt after the burial, the brothers
begin to wonder what Joseph will do now that their father is dead.

Read Genesis 50:15.

1. What were the brothers afraid of? Why do you think after
   all that had happened, they were still concerned? In your
   opinion, did Joseph have a right to hold a grudge? Why or
   why not?

   That Joseph will hate them
   + pay them back for all the
   evil he did to them.

2. If Joseph did take retributive or revengeful action, what are some things you think he could have demanded of them? In the end, what would this have accomplished? Do you think any of them would have felt better in the long run? Why or why not?

He could have sold them, commanded them to be his slaves, hurt their families (he had pwr. to do harm)

3. According to Romans 12:18–21, why shouldn't we take revenge? What should we do instead? What are some ways Joseph models the truths in these verses?

"never avenge yourselves but leave it to the wrath of God."
"Vengence is mine, I will repay, says the LORD.

4. Where have you witnessed someone other than yourself holding a grudge? What was the result for the person holding the grudge and for the person held in that grudge? Was there ever any resolution?

Holding a grudge is harboring feelings of ill-will or resentment toward another person. When we hold a grudge, it's as if we carry the offense around wherever we go so we can grab it at a moment's notice. We use this grudge to prove a point, remind someone of what they have done, or put on an armor to protect from anything that hints of similar danger. Carrying an offense in this manner is an exhausting burden and a heavy load. And ultimately, it just damages us. The person who offended us has usually moved on and we're the ones left carrying this self-imposed burden.

Now, that doesn't mean we shouldn't be wise about trusting those who have hurt us in the past. It's possible that you shouldn't stay in a relationship with someone who has wounded you deeply. It's also very likely that you should establish boundaries to help you stay healthy and safe in the future. What we're talking about here is letting go of the hold anger and resentment can impose on our hearts and souls. This isn't easy work to do. It's sometimes incredibly difficult. Especially when the offending party doesn't take any responsibility for what they have done. But it is work that can be done with the help of God and, when needed, a trusted counselor.

5. Prayerfully consider the situation and person you are seeking to forgive from this week's practice. Are there any places where you are holding on to bitterness or resentment toward this person and wishing that if only they had not done what they did, then maybe you wouldn't be experiencing this emotional pain? Look back at Romans 12:18–21. How do the truths in this passage help you begin to release some of these feelings? Pray and ask the Lord if there is anything practical you should do to help you take a step toward forgiveness. Write down any ideas that come to mind and make a plan to do one of them before the end of the week.

Before you start your lesson, take a few minutes
to review and then refine or add to your story of
naming the hurt that you are seeking to forgive.

Day 3
Avoiding, Protecting, and Grabbing

Read Genesis 50:16–17.

> 6. How did the brothers attempt to mitigate their concerns?
> Do you think Jacob gave these instructions before he died?
> Why or why not?

It's really not clear if the brothers lied in this instance. However,
I think the evidence is stacked against them. Primarily because
we find no mention of this request from Jacob anywhere in the
text. In addition, when he gives the final patriarchal blessing to
the twelve brothers in Genesis 49 would seem an obvious place to
include instructions like this. But, again, there is nothing. While
it is possible that this detail has been left out of the story, given
how important it is, it would seem like an odd omission. All this
makes me believe the brothers are lying.

Lying is incredibly tempting. It's a tactic that has been around
since the beginning of time. Adam and Eve were the very first
humans to lie when God asked them why they ate the forbidden
fruit. Adam immediately blamed Eve and Eve blamed Satan—no
one took responsibility for what had really happened (Genesis

3:10–13). The lying continues in other places in Scripture too. Some famous lies were when Abraham asked his wife Sarah to pose as his sister in an effort to preserve his life (Genesis 20), and when David slept with Bathsheba and then lied as he sent her husband to the front lines to die in an attempt to cover up his sin (2 Samuel 11). Each of these instances reveals an important aspect of why we lie. We lie to avoid the consequences of what we have done (Adam and Eve), protect what we have (Abraham), or get what we want (David and Bathsheba).

It's not just the big things that tempt us to lie, though. It's often in the little things, where a small lie feels easier, that we are most tempted.

I'm so sorry I didn't reply. I completely missed that email.

I don't think I can make it tonight; I'm not feeling well.

My boss needed me.

My kids are sick.

It was lost in the mail.

Thanks for waiting for me. The traffic was terrible.

I didn't know that was yours.

In each instance we are avoiding, protecting, or grabbing. And often we get away with it—or so we think. Which just lures us into lying again the next time.

7. If the brothers did lie to Joseph, what do you think their primary motivation was: avoiding a consequence, protecting something they had, or trying to gain something they wanted? Why do you think they struggled to trust that Joseph wouldn't be seeking revenge now that their father was gone (also consider Joseph's words in Genesis 45:5–8 and Joseph's actions over the seventeen years they had all been living in Egypt)? What do you think this ultimately says about their relationship with God and their ability to trust God?

8. Think back over the past week or two. When were you tempted to lie or even withhold or spin the truth? Reflecting on this situation, what do you think your primary reason was for being tempted to lie: avoiding a consequence, protecting something you have, or trying to gain something you wanted? If you told the lie, what happened? What could you have said that was true and what might the results have been? If you didn't tell the lie, what happened?

As you consider this question, if there is a lie you told that you feel you should go back and make amends for, consider doing that this week. As you do, remember that God forgives you for this sin as he forgives us for all of our sins. Take some time right now to talk to God about what happened. Start by confessing openly and honestly and asking him to help you see what your motivations were in telling this lie. Then in an act of repentance, which is simply turning back to God, commit to trusting him with the outcome and doing it differently next time.

"[The devil] has always hated the truth, because there is no truth in him. When he lies, it is consistent with his character; for he is a liar and the father of lies."

—John 8:44 (NLT)

9. How did Joseph respond to the message from his brothers (verse 17)? What are some of the possible reasons he responded this way?

10. When have you been lied to, and why do you think this was? When the truth came out, how did you feel? How have you been able to move forward? How has your faith in God helped you with this? If you haven't been able to move forward, why do you think this is?

If you are struggling with a situation or a person as a result of a lie, ask the Lord to help you turn this over to him. Consider entering into a process of forgiveness with the person who lied to you.

Before you start your lesson, take a
few minutes to continue the process of
forgiveness by making the intentional decision
to forgive the person who hurt you.

Day 4
Released

Read Genesis 50:18–21.

Once more the dream from Genesis 37 became a reality as the
brothers threw themselves down before Joseph. This time, in des-
peration, they offered themselves as his slaves to pay him back
for what they had done. Joseph responded in a way that was true
to his character and deep faith.

11. How do you think Joseph felt when his brothers threw
    themselves at his feet? Do you think he was tempted at all
    to make them pay for what they had done?

12. Joseph responded, "Don't be afraid," and then he asked
    them, "Am I in the place of God?" (verse 19). Why do you
    think he asked this question?

13. What did Joseph say about the brothers' intentions in Genesis 50:20? What did Joseph say about what God was able to do in spite of their intentions? What kind of internal work do you think Joseph had done with God to get to this point?

This is a very important moment in Joseph's life story. He didn't tell the brothers that what they did was good. No, he called it what it was. He named the hurt as, "You intended to harm me." Don't move past that phrase too quickly. Yes, he did move on to how God intended it for good, but he didn't gloss over the evil and sinful intentions of his brothers. This is the weight they had been carrying for years. It had been a heavy, nearly crushing burden for them. We've seen them bring it up multiple times in this story. And so, even when Joseph stated he forgave them the first time (Genesis 45:5–8), they couldn't believe it. It was just too good to be true.

I've found many of us struggle in a similar way with God's forgiveness that is extended to us. On the one hand, we very much believe in the gospel and that Jesus died for our sins—and that we are forgiven. And yet many of us still act like we need to pay God back for what we've done wrong. We try harder, serve more, and say yes to doing things we don't really want to as a feeble attempt to tip the scales back in our favor. Simply accepting his full forgiveness and being released from our just punishment feels too easy. This can leave us, just like the brothers, looking over our shoulder and wondering when we will have to pay the penalty for what we have really done. Let me reassure you. When Jesus died on the cross, he took all of your sin. All of it. There is nothing you have done or not done that wasn't covered in Jesus's death and resurrection. If you're struggling with accepting this full forgiveness, look up Ephesians 2:1–9 and Colossians 2:13–14 and write out what they say is true about you. Then make an appointment with a pastor, your small group leader, or another mature Christian to talk about God's extravagant grace, so you can start walking in the freedom he is offering you.

14. Read Romans 8:28. How does this verse compare to Genesis 50:20? Think of a hard situation that you have come through. How have you seen God take what was meant for harm and use it for good in your life? Now that you are on the other side of that circumstance, do you think the hard parts were worth what God ultimately did?

This is one of the biggest questions I've had to wrestle with regarding Joseph's story: Was it worth it? Was it worth the loss of so many years? Was it worth the imprisonment? Was it worth the slavery? Was it worth being misunderstood?

And if it had been me, would I have thought it was worth it? Would I have responded with a Joseph-like trust in God no matter the circumstances? I sure hope so. But I can't be certain, because I haven't had to face what he did. However, I can look back on many of the hard things I've experienced and see how God has used them for good in my life. That doesn't mean I want to travel those roads again or that they were any fun. But with a God-sighted perspective, I can say this life with all its ups and downs and bumps and bruises is truly worth it. And this helps me choose trust when uncertainty enters my life again.

Reflecting on Jesus and his willingness to endure terrible circumstances that ultimately led to his death also helps me choose trust.

15. Read Luke 23:32–46. This is the account of the final moments of Jesus hanging on the cross and ultimately dying. How does his death echo the truths from Genesis 50:20 and Romans 8:28? What ultimate good came out of his death (Colossians 1:21–22)? Do you think this good made his terrible death worth it? Why or why not?

Because of Joseph's faith, he maintained a God-sighted perspective. This helped him see that even the worst moments of his journey led him to the position where he had the ability to save his entire family. This understanding enabled him to fully forgive and release his brothers from what they had done.

16. How did Joseph tell the brothers they would move forward as a family (Genesis 50:21)? When he reassured them and spoke kindly to them, what are some things you think he might have said? How do you think this shows that he fully released them and forgave them? How do you think these words and actions of Joseph might have positively impacted the brothers' relationships with God?

17. Read Ephesians 4:32. How does showing kindness and compassion to others help in the process of forgiveness? How do you see Joseph do this?

How does remembering that you are forgiven help you as you continue your process of forgiving?

What are some ways you can show kindness to or have compassion for the person you are seeking to forgive?

PRACTICE REMINDER

Before you start your lesson, take a
few minutes to continue the process of
forgiveness by making the intentional decision
to forgive the person who hurt you.

Day 5
Finishing Well

Read Genesis 50:22–26.

In this passage, we come to the very end of Joseph's life. He
lived to be one hundred and ten years old, which means he
lived a little more than fifty years after Jacob died. When we
look back over Joseph's long life, we see a thirteen-year-long
blip of dark and hard circumstances. It started when he was
sold at seventeen and ended with his elevation to authority and
leadership under Pharaoh at thirty. We would never wish those
thirteen years on anyone. And yet, when we pull back, we see
that his life was so much bigger than the hard parts. Those thirteen years were real, though. And they could have derailed him
to the point of uselessness, but somehow, they didn't. Joseph
not only survived the dark years but learned how to trust God
deeply and implicitly, even in the midst of them. As a result,
Joseph became a man of deep character and integrity. A man of
his word. A man who knew how to trust God and who could
forgive the unthinkable.

18. Joseph and his brothers had fifty years to reestablish their
relationship after Jacob's death. How does this passage indicate that Joseph made good on his promise to provide
for his entire family, including his brothers? What do you

think his relationship with his brothers wound up being like?

19. In his last days, Joseph reminded the brothers of the promise of God (verse 24). What did he say God would do? Why do you think Joseph needed to remind his family who would ultimately take care of them?

20. Read Exodus 13:19. In Exodus, the next book of Scripture after Genesis, the Israelites became enslaved by the Egyptians and were forced to serve them for four hundred years. God sent Moses to rescue them. How does this verse reveal that God kept his promise and also took care of Joseph's bones, as he requested? What does this show you about God and his ability to keep promises?

21. Read 2 Peter 3:8. Considering this verse and how long it took for the Lord to fulfill his promise to the nation of Israel (according to Exodus 12:40–41; 13:19), what does this reveal to you about God's timing? Write down one or two ways that you saw God's timing being best in Joseph's story. How does this truth help you trust God's timing in your own life?

22. Joseph trusted God in the midst of great uncertainty. List some areas you're unsure of in your life right now. How does knowing all of Joseph's story help you trust God in the midst of your own uncertainty?

23. What is a promise or truth about God that you have learned through this study that can help you trust God in the midst of your own uncertainty? If you need ideas, you can look back over the previous lessons or consider one of these verses: Genesis 50:20; Psalm 34:8, 145:8; Jeremiah 29:11; or Romans 8:28.

24. Write out the promise or truth from the previous question as if it were written from God directly to you. Use your name to make it personal. For example, if I chose Romans 8:28 I might write something like, "Jodie, I am working in the midst of this hard season for your good. You can trust me and my purposes." Note that my example is pretty general. I encourage you to be more specific about the situation in your life you are seeking to apply this truth to.

Once you have your promise written out, find a notecard or sticky note and write it again. Place it somewhere you will see it to help you remember you can trust God, even in the midst of your uncertainty.

25. Genesis 50:26 states that Joseph died and was placed in a coffin. If you had to write an epitaph to place on his coffin, how would you summarize his life in just a few words?

PRACTICE REFLECTION

1. Were you able this week to move through the process of forgiveness with someone who has hurt you? If so, which step of the process was most helpful for you: writing/telling the story, naming the hurt, granting forgiveness, or releasing or renewing the relationship? Which step was hardest? If you got stuck, why do you think that is?

2. How did it help you to reflect on Joseph's extraordinary act of forgiveness to his brothers as you sought to forgive?

3. How did it help to reflect on Jesus's forgiveness toward you as you sought to forgive?

Well done, my friend! I'm so proud of you for finishing this journey well. Especially if you went through the hard process of forgiving this week. I know how difficult and painful that process can be. But I also know the incredible freedom you will find on the other side. If you are still in the process of forgiving, give yourself some grace, but don't give up. Freedom awaits you.

I also hope that you will take some of Joseph's story with you as you continue to follow God's leading in your life. There will be many times when things won't make sense to us. When life seems to be overflowing with uncertainty. When these times come, think back to your ancient brother Joseph and his journey. I often go back to his days sitting in prison—day after day wondering and waiting. It may be a grim image, but it helps me remember that God didn't forget Joseph and he has not forgotten me. He has not forgotten you either. He is working. Always working. We can trust this truth. The days may be uncertain, but our God is not. May you trust boldly as you continue following him, even in uncertainty.

ACKNOWLEDGMENTS

Thank you to my ancient brother Joseph. Your faithful and steadfast trust in God inspires me. I trust him more because of your example.

Thank you to my faithful friends who read the rough draft and offered thoughtful suggestions. Candice, Tiffany, and Sissy—this study is truly better because of you. Each of you encouraged me and helped me persevere from a blank page to a finished manuscript.

Thank you to the women of Irving Bible Church. I'm grateful I get to study God's Word with you. You inspire me, push me, and challenge me. I'm so grateful. Thank you also to Barry and Bryan for supporting me as I carved out space to write. I'm thankful you believe the sacrifice is worth it. You, brothers, are a gift to me.

Thank you to the amazing editing team at Kregel—Janyre, Sarah, and Joel. I still feel like someone is going to pinch me and wake me up from this fun dream of working and collaborating with you.

Thank you to Tim, Taylor, and Billie. You're my loves and my favorites, period. (Don't tell Ryder and Daisy.)

And mostly, thank you to Jesus. You are worthy of all my trust.

NOTES

Week 1: Favored to Forsaken

1. Nancy Guthrie, *The Promised One: Seeing Jesus in Genesis* (Wheaton, IL: Crossway, 2011), 241.
2. Timothy Keller, *Walking with God Through Pain and Suffering* (New York: Penguin, 2013), 267.

Week 2: Turning from Temptation

1. Nicole Unice, *The Struggle Is Real: Getting Better at Life, Stronger in Faith, and Free from the Stuff Keeping You Stuck* (Carol Stream, IL: Tyndale Momentum, 2018), 64.
2. D. A. Carson, *For the Love of God: A Daily Companion for Discovering the Riches of God's Word*, vol. 1 (Wheaton, IL: Crossway, 1998), 37.

Week 3: Forgotten

1. "Yousef Nadarkhani," PrisonerAlert, accessed May 7, 2021, https://www.prisoneralert.com/286.
2. Charles R. Swindoll, *Joseph: A Man of Integrity and Forgiveness* (Nashville: Thomas Nelson, 1998), 39.
3. Note from Genesis 40:6. NET Bible® copyright © 1996–2017 by Biblical Studies Press, LLC, http://netbible.com. All rights reserved. Used by permission.
4. Corrie ten Boom, *The Hiding Place* (Grand Rapids: Chosen Books, 2006), 12.

Week 4: Remembered and Restored

1. Timothy Keller, *Prayer: Experiencing Awe and Intimacy with God* (New York: Dutton, 2014), 228.

2. Nancy Guthrie, *The Promised One: Seeing Jesus in Genesis* (Wheaton, IL: Crossway, 2011), 244.

Week 5: The Weight of Sin

1. Ann Voskamp, *One Thousand Gifts: A Dare to Live Fully Right Where You Are* (Grand Rapids: Zondervan, 2010), 175.
2. C. S. Lewis, *God in the Dock* (Grand Rapids: Eerdmans, 2014), 41.

Week 6: The Test

1. Corrie ten Boom, *Jesus Is Victor* (Grand Rapids: Revell, 1985), 60.

Week 7: In God's Time

1. Max Lucado, *You'll Get Through This: Hope and Help for Your Turbulent Times* (Nashville: Thomas Nelson, 2013), 147.
2. Note on Genesis 45:24. NET Bible® copyright © 1996–2017 by Biblical Studies Press, LLC, http://netbible.com. All rights reserved. Used by permission.
3. John H. Walton, *Genesis*, NIV Application Commentary (Grand Rapids: Zondervan, 2001), 709.

Week 8: Final and Full Forgiveness

1. "What Is Forgiveness?," *Greater Good*, accessed May 7, 2021, https://greatergood.berkeley.edu/topic/forgiveness/definition.
2. Brené Brown, *Rising Strong: How the Ability to Reset Transforms the Way We Live, Love, Parent, and Lead* (New York: Spiegel & Grau, 2015), 151.
3. Max Lucado, *You'll Get Through This: Hope and Help for Your Turbulent Times* (Nashville: Thomas Nelson, 2013), 117.

ABOUT THE AUTHOR

Jodie Niznik has served in pastoral ministry for more than twelve years. Her calling and passion is to equip people to take the next step in their journey with Jesus. She loves to write about and teach scriptural truths in practical and easy-to-understand ways.

Jodie has an undergraduate degree in broadcast journalism from the University of Colorado and a master's degree in Christian education with an emphasis in women's ministry from Dallas Theological Seminary. She is also the author of *Choose: A Study of Moses for a Life That Matters* and *Crossroads: A Study of Esther and Jonah for Boldly Responding to Your Call*, and the coauthor of *Galatians: Discovering Freedom in Christ Through Daily Practice* with Sue Edwards.

Jodie is married to Tim. They have two young adult daughters, Taylor and Billie. Jodie and Tim miss their daughters but love their quiet Saturdays. Jodie believes gummy bears and coffee are sweet gifts from the Lord that provide fuel as she writes Bible studies and prepares biblical teachings.